Expressive Writing 2
A Direct Instruction Program
Workbook

Siegfried Engelmann

Jerry Silbert

Columbus, OH

The McGraw·Hill Companies

SRAonline.com

 **SRA**

2008 Imprint
Copyright © 2005 by SRA/McGraw-Hill.

Send all inquiries to:
SRA/McGraw-Hill
4400 Easton Commons
Columbus, OH 43219

Printed in the United States of America.

ISBN 0-07-603590-5

6 7 8 9 QPD 11 10 09

Part A

1. The boy was from New York.	reports	does not report
2. A boy sat on the dock and fished.	reports	does not report
3. The boy wanted to be a boxer.	reports	does not report
4. The girl wore a red swimsuit.	reports	does not report
5. The girl sat in an inner tube.	reports	does not report
6. The girl liked to swim.	reports	does not report
7. The water was very warm.	reports	does not report
8. Several fish fell out of the bucket.	reports	does not report

Part B

1. jump _____   3. bark _____   5. pick _____

2. pull _____   4. push _____   6. burn _____

Part C

1. find	*found*	6. buy		11. dig	
2. give	*gave*	7. find		12. buy	
3. buy	*bought*	8. dig		13. has	
4. dig	*dug*	9. has		14. give	
5. has	*had*	10. give		15. find	

Part D

1. _____ ran into the room.

2. _____ stood behind his desk.

3. _____ made marks on a piece of paper.

4. _____ watched the alligator from the front row.

2　　Prelesson 1

Part E

Instructions: Underline the part of each sentence that names.

An old cowboy went to town.

That cowboy rode his horse to town.

He went to town to buy food.

He rode his horse to the food store.

The cowboy went inside.

He bought the food that he needed.

Part F
1. Maria and her sister went to the store.
2. My friend had a cold.
3. The class went to the lunchroom.
4. His bike had a flat tire.

Part A

Mrs. Lee

1. Mrs. Lee talked to her sister.   reports   does not report

2. The baby sat on a rug.   reports   does not report

3. The baby had just learned how to walk.   reports   does not report

4. The cat reached toward the birdcage.   reports   does not report

5. The cat was seven years old.   reports   does not report

6. The dog liked to play with the baby.   reports   does not report

7. The baby held on to the dog's tail.   reports   does not report

8. Mrs. Lee was making a birthday cake.   reports   does not report

Part B

Instructions: Underline the part of each sentence that names.

A little gray cat looked for its owner. It looked and looked. The poor cat was hungry. The cat made a lot of noise. It went up one street and down another. The cat found its owner. That little cat felt very happy.

Part C

Instructions: Fill in each blank with *he, she* or *it.*

1. The car broke down.

2. The dream went on for an hour.

3. The young boy sat in a chair.

4. The monkey was laughing.

5. My older sister helped me.

6. The pen fell off the table.

1. _____ broke down.

2. _____ went on for an hour.

3. _____ sat in a chair.

4. _____ was laughing.

5. _____ helped me.

6. _____ fell off the table.

Part D

1.

The firefighter

- The firefighter is chopping a hole in the door.
- The firefighter was chopping a hole in the door.
- The firefighter chopped a hole in the door.

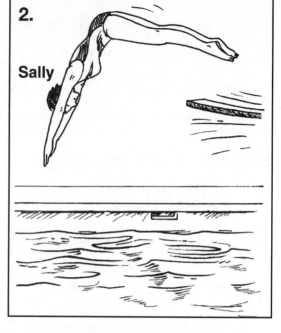

2.

Sally

- Sally is diving into the pool.
- Sally dove into the pool.
- Sally was diving into the pool.

3.

Latrell

- Latrell ate a sandwich.
- Latrell was eating a sandwich.
- Latrell is eating a sandwich.

4.

The girl

- The girl was painting the wall.
- The girl is painting the wall.
- The girl painted the wall.

6   Prelesson 2

Part E

1. The boy was eating lunch.

2. The girl is running home.

3. The man was playing soccer.

4. He is drinking water.

5. She was driving a bus.

drank	drove	ate	played	ran

	Part F
	Pedro had a very smart
	dog. The dog could do many
	tricks. It could walk on its
	back legs. It could jump
	through a hoop. All of the
	children liked to play with the
	smart dog.

Part A

Instructions: Fill in each blank with *he, she* or *it*.

1. The shirt was covered with dirt.	1. _____ was covered with dirt.
2. The rubber ball fell off the table.	2. _____ fell off the table.
3. The man sat in a chair.	3. _____ sat in a chair.
4. The book was very funny.	4. _____ was very funny.
5. The young woman rode a bike.	5. _____ rode a bike.
6. The game ended at four o'clock.	6. _____ ended at four o'clock.

Part B

Instructions: Underline the part of each sentence that names.

An old red bike sat in the yard for years. That bike became rusty. It had spider webs on the wheels. A girl decided to fix up the bike. She painted the bike bright red. She put new tires on the bike. The bike looked great. The girl liked the bike.

Part C

A bull chased Pam through a field. Pam jumped over a fence. And then the bull jumped over the fence. And Pam kept on running. And the bull was right behind her. Pam ran over to a tree. And then she climbed up the tree as fast as she could. And the bull waited under the tree until the sun went down. And then Pam climbed down after the bull left. And she knew she shouldn't have taken a shortcut through that field.

Part D

Instructions: Fix up each sentence so that it tells what the person or thing did.

1. He was taking a bath.

2. They were looking at the sky.

3. The dog was licking my face.

4. She is building a fire.

5. The teacher was sitting on a chair.

6. She is folding the paper.

built	folded	licked	looked	sat	took

Part E

1.

Norma

- Norma was sawing a board.
- Norma is sawing a board.
- Norma sawed a board.

2.

Yancy

- Yancy was trying to ride a horse.
- Yancy tried to ride a horse.
- Yancy is trying to ride a horse.

Prelesson 3   **9**

Part F

Instructions: Write sentences that report on the main thing each person did.

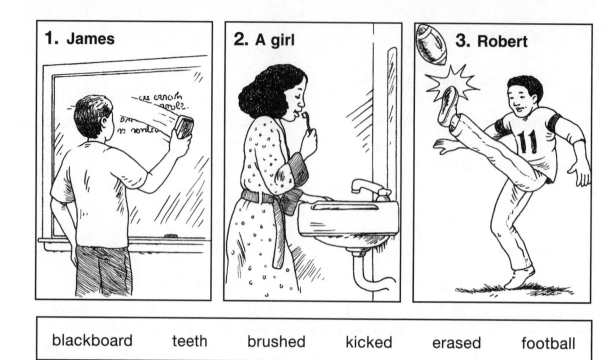

1. James
2. A girl
3. Robert

| blackboard | teeth | brushed | kicked | erased | football |

Part G

> Part G
>
>   Jason had a bad day. He missed breakfast because he woke up late. He had to walk to school in the rain.
>
> 1   2   3

Check 1: Does each sentence begin with a capital and end with a period?

Check 2: Did you spell all the words correctly?

Check 3: Did you indent the first line and start all the other lines at the margin?

Prelesson 4

Part A

Instructions: Underline the part of each sentence that names.

A hungry little cat walked into a restaurant. It wanted something to eat. A nice woman owned the restaurant. She gave the cat a bowl of milk. The little animal drank every drop of milk. The woman liked the cat. She made a little bed for it. The cat had a new home.

Part B

Tom threw a snowball at his friend. And it hit his friend's leg. And then his friend chased him. And they both ran as fast as they could. His friend caught Tom in the middle of the park. And then Tom told his friend that he was sorry for hitting him in the leg with the snowball. The boys shook hands. And they were still friends.

Part C

Instructions: Fill in the blank next to each sentence with *he, she, it* or *they.*

1. The man and the woman ate lunch.

1. _____ ate lunch.

2. Latrell and Kedrick walked on the sand.

2. _____ walked on the sand.

3. The truck had a flat tire.

3. _____ had a flat tire.

4. The apples cost 84 cents.

4. _____ cost 84 cents.

5. The women wore red shirts.

5. _____ wore red shirts.

6. The old book was worth a lot of money.

6. _____ was worth a lot of money.

7. Alberto and his dog went jogging.

7. _____ went jogging.

8. The old man wore a long blue coat.

8. _____ wore a long blue coat.

Prelesson 4   **11**

Part D

Instructions: Fix up each sentence so that it tells what the persons did.

1. She is riding a horse.

2. The girls were talking loudly.

3. The men are painting the room.

4. He was holding the baby.

5. She is standing on a chair.

6. They were washing the windows.

held	painted	rode	stood	talked	washed

Part E

Instructions: Fix up the passage so that all the sentences tell what the person did.

Marcus woke up late. He was running down the stairs. He grabbed his school book. He is jumping onto his bike. He rode the bike as fast as he could. He was parking the bike. He ran into the classroom. He was sitting in his chair.

Part F

Instructions: Write a paragraph that reports on what happened.

1. The cowboy

2. The bull

3. A clown

4. The bull   5. The clown

fell	ground	charged	ran	toward
barrel	front	hit	knocked	air
	helped	walk	away	

Check 1: Does each sentence begin with a capital and end with a period?

Check 2: Does each sentence tell what a person or thing did, not what a person or thing was doing?

Check 3: Does each sentence report on the main thing a person or thing did?

Part A

Instructions: Put in the capitals and periods. Underline the part of each sentence that names.

A young boy threw a ball the ball went over his friend's head it rolled into the street a big truck ran over the ball the truck driver gave the boys a new ball they thanked the truck driver

Part B

1. The workers fixed the house and two carpenters nailed boards over the broken windows and a plumber repaired the broken sink.

2. The girls rode their bikes to school and their friends took the bus to school and everyone arrived at school on time.

3. The telephone rang six times and nobody heard it and everybody was outside in the yard.

Part C

Instructions: Fix up each sentence so that it tells what the persons did.

1. They were wearing helmets.

2. She was throwing the ball.

3. They were cleaning the room.

4. The boys were sitting on the floor.

5. He was wearing a new shirt.

6. The clown was rubbing his nose.

sat	threw	rubbed	wore	cleaned

Part D

Instructions: Fix up the passage so that all the sentences tell what the person did, not what the person was doing.

Jerry heard a noise. He was seeing a little kitten on the sidewalk. He picked up the kitten. He was taking it home with him. He was giving it some water. He made a little bed for it. He loved his new pet.

Part E

Instructions: Fill in the blank next to each sentence with *he, she, it* or *they.*

1. A cat and a dog made a mess.

1. _____ made a mess.

2. The girls went to school.

2. _____ went to school.

3. My mother was very pretty.

3. _____ was very pretty.

4. Rodney and his brother were not home.

4. _____ were not home.

5. Four ducks swam on the lake.

5. _____ swam on the lake.

6. The tables were old.

6. _____ were old.

7. My brother came home late.

7. _____ came home late.

8. That car was bright red.

8. _____ was bright red.

Part F

Instructions: Write a paragraph that reports on what happened. Write sentences that tell the main thing each numbered person or thing did.

1. A little bird

2. James

3. His sister

4. James

5. She

bird	helped	fell	its nest	ground
	climbed	tree	branch	

Check 1: Does each sentence begin with a capital and end with a period?

Check 2: Does each sentence tell what a person or thing did, not what a person or thing was doing?

Check 3: Does each sentence first name, then report on the main thing a person or thing did?

Check 4: Did you indent the first line and start all the other lines at the margin?

Part A

Instructions: Put in the capitals and periods.

	a boy took his mom to the
	movies he had a good time the
	movie was very funny his mom
	bought a big box of popcorn they
	rode home on their bikes
	.

Part B

Instructions: Fix up the passage so that no sentence begins with *and* or *and then.*

Richard had a good day. Richard's teacher gave Richard his report card just before the school day ended. And Richard jumped with joy when he saw the good marks on his report card. And then he ran home to show his mother the report card. And then he gave her the report card. And then his mother read the report card for several minutes. And she was so happy that she made Richard a big pizza for dinner.

Part C

Instructions: Fix up the run-on sentences.

1. The boy ran down the street and he held his books in his arms.

2. The girl ran into the room and she looked all over for her books and she didn't know where they could be.

3. The airplane flew above the clouds and it was about 60 miles from the airport and the pilot looked at the charts.

4. The boy walked slowly to the store and he stopped three times to talk to his friends and the store was closed when the boy got there.

5. Rosa wrote a funny story about alligators and she read it to the class and the children liked her story very much.

6. The dog did a trick and it walked in circles on its back legs and the boy gave the dog a snack for doing such a good trick.

Part D

Instructions: Rewrite each sentence so that it tells what the person or thing did.

1. The boy was chasing a dog.
2. The girl was washing the car.
3. He was writing a letter.
4. She was eating apples.
5. The airplane was taking off.

took	chased	wrote	ate	washed

Part E

Instructions: Write a paragraph that reports on what happened. Write sentences that tell the main thing each numbered person did.

football	threw	jumped	Ramon's leg	dove
goal line	caught	tackled	grabbed	

Check 1: Does each sentence begin with a capital and end with a period?

Check 2: Does each sentence tell what a person did, not what a person was doing?

Check 3: Does each sentence first name, then report on the main thing that person did?

Check 4: Did you indent the first line and start all the other lines at the margin?

Part A

Instructions: Put in the capitals and periods.

	a girl threw a ball to her brother she threw the ball too hard it rolled into the street the boy started to run into the street a truck moved toward the boy a woman saw the truck she grabbed the boy the truck ran over the ball the woman told the boy to be more careful

Part B

Instructions: Fill in the blanks with *he, she* or *it.*

1. Robert spent all morning cleaning his room. _____ put his dirty clothes into the laundry basket. _____ washed the floor and the windows.

2. My sister went to the park. _____ played basketball with her friends for two hours. _____ scored 20 points.

3. The boat went around the small lake. _____ had three sails. _____ moved very quickly across the water.

Part C

1. Alberto ate lunch in the kitchen and he ate two cheese sandwiches covered with mustard and he got mustard all over his face and shirt.

2. The girl looked out the window at the snow and she did not like cold weather and she wished that she lived in a warmer place.

3. The dog ran down the street and it barked at a truck and the truck driver waved at the dog.

4. My friend did not feel well and she had a fever and her mother kept her home from school.

5. The dish fell off the table and it broke into many pieces and the boy swept up the pieces.

6. Rodney listened to the voice on the telephone and he didn't know who was speaking and the voice sounded strange.

Part D

Instructions: Rewrite each sentence so that it tells what the persons did.

1. The men were telling jokes.
2. She was picking up the pencils.
3. They were washing the car.
4. He was sitting on a log.
5. She was painting the wall.

| painted | told | sat | washed | picked |

Part E

Instructions: Write a paragraph that reports on what happened.

barrel	rolled	truck	rock	crashed	hill
apple	tree	teacher	boy	caught	

Check 1: Does each sentence begin with a capital and end with a period?

Check 2: Does each sentence tell what a person or thing did, not what a person or thing was doing?

Check 3: Does each sentence first name, then report on the main thing that person or thing did?

Check 4: Did you tell all the important things that happened?

Part A

Instructions: Fix up the run-on sentences in this passage.

A girl got a big dog for her birthday and the dog was so big that it could not fit through the doors of the girl's house. It had to live outside. The dog followed the girl to the school bus stop one morning and the girl didn't see the dog behind her and the dog tried to sneak onto the bus. The door of the bus was too small. The dog got stuck and all the children had to push together to get the dog off the bus.

Part B

Instructions: Fix up the passage so that each sentence begins with a capital and ends with a period.

	a man took a big egg out of a nest. The man brought the egg to his house he thought that the egg might be worth a lot of money. The doorbell rang the man walked to the door. He opened the door a big bird flew into the room. It picked up the egg the man fainted. The big bird flew away with the egg

Part C

Part D

Instructions: Edit the passage for these checks:

Check 1: Do any sentences begin with *and* or *and then?*
Check 2: Do all the words that are part of a person's name begin with a capital?

tonya jackson was playing baseball. And her team was losing two to one. tonya was at bat. The pitcher threw the ball to tonya. tonya swung. She missed the ball. And tonya was mad. The pitcher threw the ball toward Tonya again. And then Tonya swung. She hit the ball. And it went far over everybody's head. Tonya ran around the bases. Her team won the game. And then all the girls clapped for tonya.

Part E

Instructions: Cross out some of the names and write *he, she* or *it.*

Ⓐ Mario found many things when he went walking. Ⓑ Mario once found a striped cat. Ⓒ That cat was very thin. Ⓓ That cat was sitting on the sidewalk. Ⓔ Mario took the cat home with him. Ⓕ Mario tried to hide the cat from his family. Ⓖ His mother heard the cat. Ⓗ His mother liked the cat and told Mario that he could keep it.

Part F

gorilla	walked	bananas	jumped	bounced
trail	cage	picked	closed	door
gate	escaped	followed	zookeeper	people

Check 1: Does each sentence begin with a capital and end with a period?

Check 2: Does each sentence tell what the person or thing did, not what the person or thing was doing?

Check 3: Does each sentence first name, then report on the main thing that person or thing did?

Check 4: Did you tell all the important things that happened?

Prelesson 8 **25**

Part A

Instructions: Fix up the run-on sentences in this passage.

Tom made some chocolate cookies and he put them in a shoe box and he put the shoe box in a corner of the kitchen. He went outside to play. Susan started cleaning the kitchen and she did not know what was in the shoe box and she threw the shoe box away. Tom got hungry. He went into the kitchen. He looked for the shoe box. It was gone. He asked Susan if she had seen the shoe box and she told him she had thrown it away. Tom told Susan what was in the shoe box. Susan helped Tom make another batch of cookies.

Part B

Instructions: Cross out some of the names and write *he, she* or *it.*

Ⓐ Trina loved to look for things on the sidewalk. Ⓑ Trina found three bugs, two rocks and a baseball yesterday. Ⓒ Her father did not like some of the things she found. Ⓓ Her father did not like the bugs that Trina brought home. Ⓔ Trina's brother liked one of the things she found. Ⓕ Trina's brother liked the baseball.

Part C

Instructions: Fix up the passage so that each sentence begins with a capital and ends with a period.

	a man saw a butterfly it had purple and white spots. The man wanted to catch the butterfly he got a net. He started to chase the butterfly it flew over a pond. The man fell into the pond the pretty butterfly flew away

Part D

Instructions: If the words are somebody's name, begin the words with capital letters.

lamar jenkins	mrs. williams	the doctor	his brother
tyrell washington	jerry martinez	this boy	mr. garcia
the girl	the nurse	mrs. cash	

Part E

Instructions: Fix up the passage so that all the sentences tell what a person did, not what a person was doing.

Shameka bought a little tree. She was digging a hole in her yard. She put the tree into the hole. She was filling the hole with dirt. She was watering the tree. She built a little fence around the tree.

Part F

Instructions: Write a paragraph that reports on what happened.

candle	shelf	pile of newspapers	jumped
fell	woman	pail	poured	fire
	picked up	knocked	burn	

Check 1: Are there any run-on sentences in your paragraph?

Check 2: Does each sentence begin with a capital and end with a period?

Check 3: Did you tell all the important things that must have happened?

Part A

Instructions: Fix up the run-on sentences in this passage.

A man went fishing at the lake and he rowed his boat out into the middle of the lake and he thought about eating fish that night for dinner. A fish saw the man's fishing line. The fish did not want to be eaten and it decided to fool the fisherman and it hooked an old shoe onto the end of the fishing line. The fisherman pulled the line up and he thought that a fish was on the line and he was angry when he saw the old shoe. The fisherman threw his line back into the water and the fish fooled him again. It hooked an old tire onto the fisherman's line. The fisherman pulled up the line and he was very angry when he saw the tire. The fisherman rowed back to shore and went home.

Part B

Instructions: Edit the passage for these checks:

Check 1: Do any sentences begin with *and* or *and then?*
Check 2: Does each word that is a person's name begin with a capital?

Ellen and her brother wanted to build a bench. They bought a book about building benches. And then ellen bought some wood. And then her brother sawed the wood into small pieces. They nailed the pieces together very carefully. And ellen made sure that no nails were sticking out of the wood. And they painted the bench red, white and blue.

Part C

Instructions: Cross out some of the names, and write *he, she* or *it.*

James had a birthday yesterday. James was 35 years old. His mother brought a big birthday cake to his office. His mother gave a piece of cake to each person in the office. The cake tasted great. The cake had chocolate icing.

Part D

Instructions: Fix up the passage so that each sentence begins with a capital and ends with a period.

	a man went for a walk he
	found a huge egg. He brought
	the egg home the egg started to
	crack. A huge reptile came out
	of the egg it flew around the
	man's house. It knocked over
	chairs and tables it wrecked
	the room. The man opened all
	the windows. The huge reptile
	flew out of the house. The man
	cleaned up the mess.

30   Prelesson 10

Part E

Instructions: Write a paragraph that reports on what happened.

tried	fly	flyswatter	flew	landed
window		cherries	baker	missed
wiped	face	splattered	apron	cleaned

Check 1: Are there any run-on sentences in your paragraph?

Check 2: Does each sentence begin with a capital and end with a period?

Check 3: Did you tell all the important things that must have happened?

Test Part A

Instructions: Fix up the passage so that all the sentences tell what the person did, not what the person was doing.

Marcus woke up late. He was running down the stairs. He grabbed his school book. He was jumping onto his bike. He rode the bike as fast as he could. He was parking the bike. He ran into the classroom. He was sitting in his chair.

Test Part B

Instructions: Fix up the run-on sentences in this passage.

A boy threw a stick at a butterfly and the stick missed the butterfly. The stick went into a bush. The boy walked toward the bush. He wanted to get the stick. The bush started to shake and the boy stopped walking and a funny looking animal walked out from behind the bush. The animal had a big white stripe down its back. The animal was a skunk. It was mad. The stick had hit the skunk. The skunk made a terrible smell and the boy spent hours in the bathtub that night. The boy never forgot that day.

Test Part C

Instructions: Put in the capitals and periods.

a woman went to the zoo she watched the monkeys do tricks a big monkey stood on its head the woman took a picture of the big monkey she showed the picture to her grandchildren they liked the picture

Test Part D

Instructions: Cross out some of the names and write *he, she* or *it.*

My friends loved to read books. Jill had just finished a book about dinosaurs. Jill could name 20 different dinosaurs. Tom liked books about space. Tom had just finished a book about the stars. The book belonged to his uncle. The book had 999 pages.

Test Part E

Instructions: Write a paragraph that reports on what happened.

Ricky

threw	hornets' nest	rock	fell	branch
	pond	chased	flew	jumped	ground

Check 1: Are there any run-on sentences in your paragraph?

Check 2: Does each sentence begin with a capital and end with a period?

Check 3: Does each sentence first name, then tell what that person or thing did?

Check 4: Did you tell all the important things that must have happened?

Part A

1. He went to the store <u>after dinner</u>.

2. She fell asleep <u>before the movie ended</u>.

3. A bird started to sing <u>when the rain stopped</u>.

4. The boy cleaned the garage after he ate breakfast.

5. Four robins went to sleep before the sun went down.

6. Ann fixed her car yesterday morning.

7. She brushed her teeth after she washed her face.

8. The people clapped when the movie ended.

Part B

Instructions: Fix up the passage so that no sentence begins with *and* or *and then*.

Nancy and her dad drove home after Nancy's last class at Sheldon High School. And they drove down a very steep street. And then Nancy's dad parked the car in front of an ice cream store. He went into the store to buy ice cream while Nancy waited in the car. And the car began to roll down the steep hill. Nancy's dad saw the car rolling away with Nancy. And he ran out of the store, but he couldn't catch up to the car. And Nancy was scared. People in the street jumped to get out of the way of the car. Nancy took hold of the steering wheel. She steered the car all the way to the bottom of the steep hill. And she kept the car from hitting any cars or people. And Nancy's dad was very proud.

Part C

Instructions: Fix up the run-on sentences.

1. Ana hit the ball very hard and the ball went over the fence and the kids cheered for Ana.

2. A man got out of his car and it had a flat tire and the man was not very happy.

3. Tom watched the boats sail up the river and his favorite boat went by at about three o'clock and it had two big blue sails.

Part D

1. The girls <u>play</u> baseball.

2. My little brother <u>has</u> a cold.

3. The show <u>starts</u> 10 minutes late.

4. They <u>go</u> home early.

5. The teacher <u>gives</u> a star to Joe.

6. They <u>run</u> two miles every day.

7. The game <u>is</u> over.

8. Tina <u>has</u> two dollars.

Part E

Instructions: Write a paragraph that tells what happened. Tell what the people or things did, but don't tell what anybody said.

lightning bolt	cloudy	bridge	collapsed	blanket
road	stopped	painted	flames	burned	wrote

Check 1: Are there any run-on sentences in your paragraph?

Check 2: Does each sentence begin with a capital, end with a period and tell what happened?

Check 3: Did you tell all the important things that must have happened?

Check 4: Did you end your paragraph by telling what the last picture shows?

Lesson 2

Part A

Instructions: Change each sentence so that it tells what happened.

1. Four people go to the beach.

2. The women play softball.

3. The red bird has a twig in its mouth.

4. Marcus is taller than Alan.

5. Rosa pulls the wagon behind her bike.

Part B

Instructions: Put in the capitals and periods.

	The women fixed up an old car they made the car look brand new mary put a new engine into the car she also fixed the brakes her sister painted the outside of the car they sold the car for 900 dollars they used the money to buy a new motorcycle

Part C

1. Tyrell picked up the phone <u>after it rang six times</u>.

2. Two trees fell down <u>during the storm</u>.

3. The baby started to cry when his mother walked out of the room.

4. Tom finished his homework at three o'clock in the morning.

5. The boy cleaned his room while his mother went shopping.

6. They shook hands after the game ended.

7. We went to the movies last night.

Part D

Instructions: Fix up the run-on sentences.

Gwen loved to teach tricks to her horse and that horse learned new tricks quickly and it had already learned many tricks. It was able to count by nodding its head. It was able to roll over and the young teacher was proud of her horse and she thought it was the smartest horse in the world.

Part E

	1. Marla said, "Climbing trees is fun."
	2. Tom said, "
	3. Oscar said,

Lesson 2   **39**

Part F

Instructions: Write a paragraph that tells what happened. Tell what the people or things did, but don't tell what anybody said.

Betty's cat

Betty

firefighter

| telephone | birdcage | flew | window | climbed |
| fire department | | grabbed | ladder | rescued |

Check 1: Are there any run-on sentences in your paragraph?

Check 2: Does each sentence begin with a capital, end with a period and tell what happened?

Check 3: Did you tell all the important things that must have happened?

Check 4: Did you end your paragraph by telling what the last picture shows?

Part A

1. He brushed his teeth after he washed his face.

2. We did our math in the morning.

3. The engine made a funny noise before the car stopped.

4. Latrell read a book while he waited for his brother.

5. Alicia bought a new shirt yesterday afternoon.

Part B

Instructions: Fix up the passage so it is punctuated correctly.

	Sharon built a raft and she took the raft to a lake and a boy was standing on a dock next to the lake. The boy fell into the water and he couldn't swim. He started to sink and Sharon threw her raft into the lake. It floated right next to the boy and he climbed onto the raft and he paddled the raft back to shore.

Part C

1.	*Maria said,*
2.	*The teacher said,*
3.	*Vince said,*

Part D

Instructions: Rewrite each sentence so that it begins with the part that tells when.

1. He went to the store after dinner.
2. She fell asleep before the movie ended.
3. We walked home when the rain stopped.
4. He read a book in the morning.

Part E

Instructions: Write a paragraph that tells what happened. Tell what the person or things did, but don't tell what anybody said.

A cowboy

edge	cliff	scared	tumbled	turned
around	horse's tail		plants	snake
grabbed	bucked	whistled	forward	backward

Check 1: Are there any run-on sentences in your paragraph?

Check 2: Does each sentence begin with a capital, end with a period and tell what happened?

Check 3: Did you tell all the important things that must have happened?

Check 4: Did you end your paragraph by telling what the last picture shows?

Part A

Instructions: Fix up the passage so each sentence is punctuated correctly.

A zookeeper took her little brother to the zoo they walked to the lion's cage a big lion jumped against the bars. The cage door swung open the lion started to walk out of the cage and The zookeeper threw a hamburger into the cage and it landed near the lion and the lion pounced on the hamburger the zookeeper locked the cage door while the lion gobbled down the hamburger.

Part B

He sat on his dad's lap. The circus performance had just begun. In one ring, he pulled a wagon. Bozo sat in the wagon. It trotted around the other ring. She stood on the horse's back.

Lesson 4   45

Part C

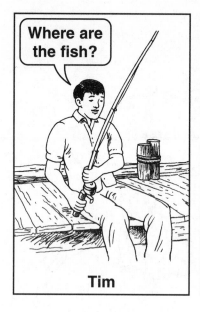

Where are the fish?

Tim

Do you like big hamburgers?

Alonzo

The first pancake is almost done.

Mr. Coleman

1.	Tim said, "Where are the fish?"
1.	Tim said,
2.	Alonzo said,
3.	Mr. Coleman said,

Part D

Instructions: Write each sentence so that it begins with the part that tells when.

1. Everybody clapped when he began to sing.
2. She took a shower after she came home from school.
3. The horse started to run when the car backfired.
4. We walked nine miles before the sun went down.

Part E

Instructions: Write a paragraph that tells what happened. Tell what the person or things did, but don't tell what anybody said.

Frisbee	bushes	barked	climbed	growled	heard
noise	scared	caught	threw	appeared	followed

Check 1: Are there any run-on sentences in your paragraph?

Check 2: Does each sentence begin with a capital, end with a period and tell what happened?

Check 3: Did you tell all the important things that must have happened?

Check 4: Did you end your paragraph by telling what the last picture shows?

	Paragraph					
Workbook	Check 1	Check 2	Check 3	Check 4	Bonus	Total

Part A

1. Desmond stood up and waved to his friend.

2. A girl jumped up and clapped her hands.

3. My friend stopped walking and waited for the light to turn green.

Part B

1. The boy ran down the street and he did not want to be late for school.

2. The boy got up and sat on his bed.

3. The girl ran back into the room and she looked for her coat and she had left her keys in her coat pocket.

4. Bill loved to bake cakes and he baked 25 cakes yesterday.

5. Ann stood up and walked to the door.

Part C

The workers were repairing it near the mountains. She sawed a big pole. She used a handsaw to cut the pole. She lifted up a pole. She held the pole with two hands. He hammered the wire onto a pole.

Part D

Instructions: Write sentences that tell what the people said.

Part E

Instructions: Write each sentence so that it begins with the part that tells when.

1. My friend went home after we finished eating dinner.
2. He lost seven pounds during the last two weeks.
3. The movie started when they sat down.

Part F

Instructions: Write a paragraph that tells what happened. Tell what the person or things did, but don't tell what anybody said.

ice	hole	water	skidded
ladder	skated	pulled	soaked
barricade	dried	scarf	licked

Check 1: Are there any run-on sentences in your paragraph?

Check 2: Does each sentence begin with a capital, end with a period and tell what happened?

★ **Check 3:** Did you tell all the important things that must have happened?

Check 4: Did you end your paragraph by telling what the last picture shows?

(★ = bonus check)

	Paragraph				★	
Workbook	Check 1	Check 2	Check 3	Check 4	Bonus	Total

Part A

Instructions: Fix up the run-on sentences.

1. Tim heard a loud noise and he ran outside and he saw a big cow standing in the grass.

2. The man picked up the ball and threw it back to the children.

3. Kelly was very excited and she knew that today was the last day of school.

4. Ana held her breath and jumped into the pool.

5. Tamika had two dogs and she liked to play with the dogs after school.

6. James walked to school in the morning and took the bus home in the afternoon.

Part B

It jumped over a fence. It had a saddle on its back. He lay on the ground. He had just fallen off the horse. He sat on a fence.

Part C

Instructions: Fix up the passage so each sentence is punctuated correctly.

A woman went fishing yesterday afternoon and she took along her little brother they fished at the pond near their house. The woman showed her brother how to put bait on his line they fished all afternoon. The woman caught six fish the boy caught five fish. They made a big fish dinner for the family that night.

Part D

Instructions: Write sentences that tell what the people said.

Part E

Instructions: Write each sentence so it begins with the part that tells when.

1. Our dog fell asleep when we turned off the radio.
2. She finished her homework before she ate lunch.
3. The man went jogging after the sun went down.

Part F

Instructions: Write a paragraph that tells what happened.

A storm came up while Tom was in his boat.

rocks

seashells

HELP

crashed	island	seashells	climbed	walked
sign	helicopter	rescue	rope ladder	
	waves	pilot		

★ **Check 1:** Is each sentence punctuated correctly?
Check 2: Did you tell all the important things that must have happened?
Check 3: Did you start your paragraph with the right sentence?
Check 4: Did you end your paragraph by telling what the last picture shows?

(★ = bonus check)

| Workbook | Paragraph | | | | ★ | |
	Check 1	Check 2	Check 3	Check 4	Bonus	Total

Part A

Instructions: Fix up the run-on sentences in this passage.

A girl picked flowers by the side of the road and she pulled up many different kinds of pretty flowers. She took the flowers home and put them in a vase by the window. The sun came through the window every morning. The girl took good care of the flowers and she made sure they had enough water. Everybody enjoyed looking at the beautiful flowers.

Part B

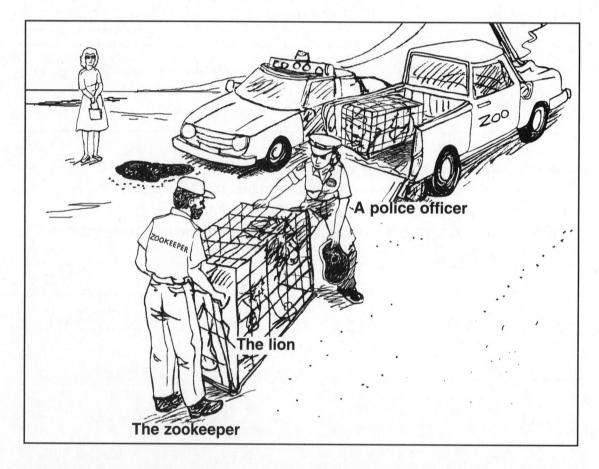

She stood in back of the cage. She held a big steak in her hands. It walked into the cage. It had its eyes on the steak. He closed the cage door as the lion walked into the cage.

Part C

Mr. James spent the day painting a picture. He stepped back to look at his picture. He heard a noise. _____①_____ The easel tilted over. Paint splattered all over the picture as the picture flew into the air.

Mrs. James came into the room. She saw the picture. She thought that Mr. James had finished the painting. She put the picture into a big box. _____②_____ Mrs. James smiled as Mr. James looked at his picture. He looked very surprised.

Part D

Instructions: Write complete sentences that tell what the people said.

Did you see my new coat?

Derek

I found your book on the floor.

Ashley

Is the dog in the house?

Lee

Lesson 7   **55**

Part E

Instructions: Write a paragraph that tells what happened.

> Kate fixed the fence while Doug took the children for a ride in the wagon.

backfired	fell	galloped	reins	pulled
jumped	horse	caught	grabbed	scared

Check 1: Is each sentence punctuated correctly?

★ **Check 2:** Did you tell all the important things that must have happened?

Check 3: Did you start your paragraph with the right sentence?

Check 4: Did you end your paragraph by telling what the last picture shows?

(★ = bonus check)

	Paragraph				★	
Workbook	Check 1	Check 2	Check 3	Check 4	Bonus	Total

Lesson 8

Part A

Instructions: Fix up the passage so that each sentence is punctuated correctly.

Nancy heard a loud noise. She got on her bike and rode over to where the noise had come from. She saw a spacecraft parked in front of a tree. Nancy got off her bike and walked toward the spacecraft. The spacecraft door opened Nancy walked into the empty spacecraft. She saw thousands of lights and buttons and Nancy was very excited she pushed a big red button the engines roared as the spacecraft lifted off the ground. Nancy looked out the window as the spacecraft flew around the earth and nobody believed Nancy when she told them about her trip in the spacecraft.

Part B

_____ talked on the phone as she stirred cake mix in the bowl.

_____ looked at a book on the table. _____ sat on the

rug. _____ held a rattle in one hand and pulled the dog's tail with his

other hand. _____ reached toward the birdcage. _____

stood on the windowsill and held on to the curtain with a paw.

Part C

A truck was carrying two lions to the zoo. The zookeeper saw a huge hole in the street. _____①_____ A cage fell off the truck. The cage door swung open. A lion walked out of the cage and chased a woman.

A police officer ran into a meat market. A butcher threw a steak to the police officer. _____②_____ The lion walked into the cage. The zookeeper closed the cage door.

Part D

Instructions: Write each sentence so that it begins with the part that tells when.

1. The children went to sleep when their mom got home.
2. Lisa cleaned the house while the baby took a nap.
3. He brushed his teeth before he went to sleep.

Part E

Instructions: Write a paragraph that tells what happened.

Troy took his dog for a walk while his big sister fixed the car.

squirrel	leaped	chased	tire	leash
stream	tied	edge	grabbed	toward	climbed

Check 1: Is each sentence punctuated correctly?

★ **Check 2:** Did you tell all the important things that must have happened?

Check 3: Did you start your paragraph with the right sentence?

Check 4: Did you end your paragraph by telling what the last picture shows?

(★ = bonus check)

	Paragraph				★	
Workbook	Check 1	Check 2	Check 3	Check 4	Bonus	Total

Lesson 9

Part A

_____ leaned against a pole on the side of the dock.

_____ held a fishing pole in one hand. _____ sat in an

inner tube. _____ wore a cap and a bathing suit. _____

sat in Doris' lap. _____ put a paw on her knee. _____

walked away with a fish in its mouth.

Part B

1. He went to the store <u>to get some cheese.</u>

2. She was sad <u>because she was sick.</u>

3. They needed ten dollars <u>to get in to the movies.</u>

4. The boy limped <u>because his leg hurt.</u>

5. She picked up the phone <u>to call her brother.</u>

6. Rafael was happy <u>because his team won the game.</u>

Part C

1	*The people were having a*
2	*good time in the park. The*
3	*women played soccer in the*
4	*field. Six women played on*
5	*each team.*
6	*The men went swimming*
7	*in the river next to the park.*
8	*The water was very cold.*

Part D

Instructions: Write complete sentences that tell the exact words the people said.

We won the game last night.

What did you say?

Where is my new book?

James

Nicole

Elisa

Part E

Mr. and Mrs. Iverson were walking in the forest when they saw something unusual.

During the night, Mr. and Mrs. Iverson heard noises coming from the garage.

| pick-up truck | brought | object | reptile |
| knocked | strange | flew | |

★ **Check 1:** Is each sentence punctuated correctly?

Check 2: Did you tell all the important things that must have happened?

Check 3: Did you end the first paragraph by telling what the first picture shows?

Check 4: Did you indent the first word of each paragraph and begin each paragraph with the right sentence?

| | Passage | | | | ★ | |
Workbook	Check 1	Check 2	Check 3	Check 4	Bonus	Total

Lesson 10

Part A

1. She was very happy <u>because she got an A in math.</u>

2. She ran as fast as she could <u>to catch the bus.</u>

3. He turned on the TV to watch his favorite show.

4. Bill got home late because he missed the bus.

Part B

_____ worked on a car engine. _____ leaned over the front of the car. _____ put gas into a car. _____ took a tire off a pickup truck. _____ bent down on his knees as he took off the tire.

Part C

Instructions: Punctuate each sentence. Make sure you follow these rules:

1. Put a comma after the word *said.*

2. Capitalize the first word the person said.

3. Put an ending mark at the end of the sentence.

4. Put quote marks around the exact words the person said.

1.	The boy said are you hungry
2.	The little girls said our cat is sick
3.	She said why did you do that
4.	He said I love ice cream

Part D

Instructions: Write each sentence so that it begins with the part that tells when.

1. She closed her eyes as she walked into the room.
2. We did our homework in the morning.
3. They talked about the movie as they walked home.

Part E

Robert was driving his Jeep next to the river.

The Jeep slid into the water.

| deer | rope | splashed | swerved | river | avoid |
| bounded | caught | climbed | threw | tied | |

Check 1: Is each sentence punctuated correctly?

Check 2: Did you tell all the important things that must have happened?

★ **Check 3:** Did you end your first paragraph by telling what the first picture shows?

Check 4: Did you indent the first word of each paragraph and begin each paragraph with the right sentence?

	Passage				★	
Workbook	Check 1	Check 2	Check 3	Check 4	Bonus	Total

Part A

Instructions: Each sentence begins with a part that tells when. Put in the comma after the part that tells when.

1. When Juan began to sing everybody clapped.

2. Before the man went to sleep he brushed his teeth.

3. During the first six minutes nobody said a word.

4. After the show ended we went to the ice cream store.

5. By the end of the week we had 10 dollars.

6. As the sky grew darker the birds started to chirp.

Part B

1. Martha played catch with Rosa.

   Martha
   She   stood near the fence.

2. Martha played catch with Marcus.

   Martha
   She   stood near the fence.

3. Tom met Jim at the bus stop.

   Tom
   He   had been downtown all day.

4. Jill waved to Trina.

   Jill
   She   was sitting in the car.

5. Ann dropped a bottle on Tom.

   Ann
   She   felt terrible.

Part C

Instructions: Punctuate each sentence. Make sure you follow these rules:

1. Put a comma after the word *said.*

2. Capitalize the first word the person said.

3. Put an ending mark at the end of the sentence.

4. Put quote marks around the exact words the person said.

1.	She said my team scored 50 points
2.	The man on the bench said is it time to go
3.	Her brother said I made hamburgers for dinner
4.	Marcus said when will it stop raining

Part D

Tim was driving his car on an icy mountain road. Rain was falling. Tim saw a huge sheet of ice on the road. He tried to stop his car. _____①_____ Tim had trouble getting out of the car.

Alice drove her truck on the same road. She saw Tim's car and stopped her truck. She grabbed a rope as she jumped out of the truck. She tied one end of the rope to a tree. _____②_____ Tim held on to the rope as he climbed up the side of the mountain.

Lesson 11   **69**

Part E

A truck was carrying two lions to the zoo.

The police officer knew this was a dangerous situation.

The police officer

The zookeeper

crashed   pole   opened   hole   street   swerved   avoid

cage   butcher   chased   steak   piece   closed

Check 1: Is each sentence punctuated correctly?

★ **Check 2:** Did you tell all the important things that must have happened?

Check 3: Did you end the first paragraph by telling what the first picture shows?

Check 4: Did you indent the first word of each paragraph and begin each paragraph with the right sentence?

Workbook	Passage				★	
	Check 1	Check 2	Check 3	Check 4	Bonus	Total

Lesson 12

Part A

Instructions: Each sentence begins with a part that tells when. Put in a comma after the part that tells when.

1. After the girls ate lunch they walked to the river.

2. Yesterday morning we washed the windows.

3. When the sun went down the birds stopped singing.

4. After we came in from gym we did our math and reading.

5. When the cowboy heard the noise he jumped onto his horse.

6. By the end of the week we had 20 points.

7. As she walked into the room she waved to her brother.

8. At last he finished painting the wall.

Part B

1. Orlando shook hands with Mary.

   Mary
   She had just won the big race.

2. Tim wanted Jerome to go home.

   Tim
   He had a lot of homework.

3. Amanda gave her sister a kitten.

   Her sister
   She loved cats.

4. Lisa took Jim out for lunch.

   Lisa
   She paid for the meal.

5. Carlos asked Ana to help him with his math.

   Carlos
   He had a lot of homework.

6. Ann and Ellen walked up the stairs.

   Ann
   She carried a package.

Part C

Instructions: Punctuate each sentence.

1.	He said we won the race
2.	She said are you feeling well
3.	The coach said everybody did a great job
4.	Bill said where is my coat

Part D

1. We had a party after the game ended.
2. The phone rang as she opened the door.
3. He woke up when the alarm clock buzzed.

Part E

Mr. James heard a loud noise just as he finished painting a picture for the art contest.

Mrs. James did not know about the accident.

| knocked over | chased | splattered | first-place ribbon |
| amazed | surprised | unique | awarded | judges |

★ **Check 1:** Is each sentence punctuated correctly?

Check 2: Did you tell all the important things that must have happened?

Check 3: Did you end the first paragraph by telling what the top picture shows?

Check 4: Did you indent the first word of each paragraph and begin each paragraph with the right sentence?

| Workbook | Passage | | | | ★ | |
	Check 1	Check 2	Check 3	Check 4	Bonus	Total

Part A

Instructions: The writer of this passage forgot to punctuate what people said. Put in the missing commas, quote marks and capital letters.

Robert bent down to talk to his dog. He said do you want to go for a run? The dog wagged its tail. Robert said go get your leash. The dog turned around. It ran out the door. It came back with the leash in its mouth. Robert said should we run by the river? The dog wagged its tail again. Robert and his dog ran 10 miles.

Part B

1. Jane did not know where Trina lived.

   Jane
   She   had just moved to the city.

2. Amanda told Tom how to fix the bike.

   Amanda
   She   had taken a bike repair class.

3. Tyrell sat next to James.

   Tyrell
   He   was the tallest boy in the class.

4. Tom couldn't find his sister in the park.

   Tom
   He   didn't know where to look next.

5. My mom gave Mark a dollar.

   My mom
   She   needed change for the washing machine.

6. My mom told Nancy to go to sleep.

   My mom
   She   was very tired.

Part C

1. When we got home, the dog started howling.
2. The air was cold in the morning.
3. After he ate lunch, he took a nap.
4. He painted a picture as he talked on the phone.

Lesson 13   **75**

Part D

Instructions: Write complete sentences that tell what the people said.

Part E

Tim drove his car on an icy mountain road.

Alice drove her truck on the same road.

| brakes | skidded | swerved | ledge | cliff | rope |
| caught | threw | climbed | tied | terrified | |

Check 1: Is each sentence punctuated correctly?

★ **Check 2:** Did you tell all the important things that must have happened?

Check 3: Did you end the first paragraph by telling what the top picture shows?

Check 4: Did you indent the first word of each paragraph and begin each paragraph with the right sentence?

	Passage				★	
Workbook	Check 1	Check 2	Check 3	Check 4	Bonus	Total

Lesson 13   **77**

Part A

Instructions: The writer of this passage forgot to punctuate what people said. Put in the missing commas, quote marks and capital letters.

Tom walked up to the little spaceman. Tom said can you speak English? The spaceman smiled. Tom said will you show me the inside of your spaceship? The spaceman took Tom inside the spaceship. The door closed. The spaceship took off. It flew high above the city. Tom said this is fantastic. After several trips around the world, the spaceship landed. Tom shook the spaceman's four hands. Tom said thank you very much.

Part B

1. Yolanda and Alicia went fishing.

   Alicia
   She   caught three big fish.

2. Tom asked Kevin to help him build a bench.

   Kevin
   He   wanted to be a carpenter.

3. Robert threw the football to Jane.

   Jane
   She   caught the ball with her left hand.

4. Lisa called Sam last night.

   Lisa
   She   told him about the new movie.

5. Sam taught Michael how to cook hamburgers.

   Sam
   He   lived by himself.

6. Alberto asked Amy about the weather.

   Alberto
   He   had been inside all day.

Part C

1. When the car started, the lights came on.
2. We watched football on Monday night.
3. After she fixed the car, she made dinner.
4. He fell asleep while he was watching TV.
5. She brushed her teeth before she went to sleep.

Part D

Jerry wanted to show his sister how well he could dribble a basketball.

His sister picked up the lamp.

table	broke	pieces	glued	garage	shook
thanked	floor	together	carried	accidentally	repaired

★ **Check 1:** Did you write sentences that tell the exact words somebody said?

Check 2: Is each sentence punctuated correctly?

Check 3: Did you tell all the important things that must have happened?

Check 4: Did you indent the first word of each paragraph and begin each paragraph with the right sentence?

	Passage				★	
Workbook	Check 1	Check 2	Check 3	Check 4	Bonus	Total

Part A

Instructions: Fix up the run-on sentences in this passage.

Ann wanted to make a big meal for her dad and it was his birthday. Ann ran home after school and went straight to the kitchen. Ann started to cook and she cooked a big meatloaf and she put the meatloaf in the refrigerator. She made a milkshake for herself. Her brother walked into the kitchen and he was carrying a big meatloaf and he had made the meatloaf at a neighbor's house. The children heard a noise at the door. Their mother walked into the room. She also had a meatloaf and they all started to laugh. The family had meatloaf for dinner. Everybody had meatloaf sandwiches for the rest of the week.

Part B

Instructions: Write complete sentences that tell what the people said.

1. Alicia **2. Tim** **3. Amanda**

Part C

Instructions: Write each sentence so it begins with the part that tells when.

1. The birds began to sing when the rain stopped.
2. We talked about school while we waited for the bus.
3. He brushed his teeth before he went to sleep.

Part D

A zookeeper was driving two lions to the zoo.

The police officer knew it was a dangerous situation.

| crashed | pole | opened | hole | street | swerved | avoid |
| cage | butcher | chased | steak | piece | closed | asked |

Check 1: Is each sentence punctuated correctly?

★ **Check 2:** Did you tell all the important things that must have happened?

Check 3: Did you end the first paragraph by telling what the top picture shows?

Check 4: Did you indent the first word of each paragraph and begin each paragraph with the right sentence?

Workbook	Passage				★	
	Check 1	Check 2	Check 3	Check 4	Bonus	Total

Lesson 16

Part A

Instructions: Each sentence begins with a part that tells when. Put a comma after the part that tells when.

1. During the first minute of the game we scored 10 points.

2. The next day we stayed at home.

3. By the time he woke up everybody had gone to work.

4. When the lights went out the dog began to bark.

5. While the children played on the swings their parents cooked dinner.

6. On Monday night we watched TV.

7. As she made dinner she sang a song.

Part B

1. Linda watched Michael draw a picture.

   Michael
   He   was a good artist.

2. Tom gave his sister a bucket of water.

   His sister
   She   threw the water onto the fire.

3. Susan showed her mother where the car was.

   Her mother
   She   had the car keys.

4. Amy stood close to her brother.

   Amy
   She   helped him cross the street.

5. Robert helped Tom make a pizza.

   Tom
   He   was very hungry.

6. Tamika taught Ana a new card trick.

   Tamika
   She   knew over 50 card tricks.

Part C

Instructions: Move the part that tells when and rewrite each sentence.

1. In the morning, we went to the park.

2. He ran home after the rain stopped.

3. She put on a hat as she walked out the door.

4. On Saturday, we stayed at home.

5. When they came home from school, they milked the cows.

Part D

Instructions: Write complete sentences that tell what the people said.

Today is my birthday. I am 16.

My gloves are missing. Have you seen them?

The rain stopped. We can go outside.

A. Yolanda   **1. James**   **2. Nicole**

A. Yolanda said, "Today is my birthday. I am 16."

Part E

Julio and Elisa wanted to do something special for their mother on her birthday.

Julio and Elisa picked up their mom at her office.

| tickets | bought | drove | enjoyed |
| delicious | bouquet of flowers | | front-row seats |

★ **Check 1:** Did you write sentences that tell the exact words somebody said?

Check 2: Is each sentence punctuated correctly?

Check 3: Did you tell all the important things that must have happened?

Check 4: Did you indent the first word of each paragraph and begin each paragraph with the right sentence?

	Passage				★	
Workbook	Check 1	Check 2	Check 3	Check 4	Bonus	Total

Lesson 16   85

Lesson 17

Part A

Instructions: Each sentence begins with a part that tells when. Put the missing comma into each sentence.

1. Before anybody knew what was happening the crooks ran out of the store.

2. Whenever he woke up late he missed the school bus.

3. When she climbed onto the roof she could see for miles.

4. As he stepped onto the scale he said, "I hope I lost some weight."

5. Early last Saturday morning they went fishing.

6. Every time he went to the store on the corner the owner gave him a piece of gum.

7. At first nobody talked to them.

Part B

_____ and _____ were swimming. _____ wore a bathing cap. _____ also wore a watch. _____ watched the two girls swim. _____ wore sunglasses. _____ sat on a blanket. _____ stood next to the blanket. _____ wore shorts. _____ read a book.

Lesson 17   **87**

Part C

Instructions: Rewrite all the sentences so that the part that tells when is moved.

1. Everybody was happy by the end of the day.
2. We finished our work before we went outside.
3. As they walked home, they talked about the movie.
4. When he woke up, he felt sick.

Part D

Instructions: Write complete sentences that tell what the people said.

1. Travis   2. My friend   3. Yolanda

Part E

Brittany was hungry when she came home from work.

Where is all the food I bought?

her brothers

Brittany went shopping for more food.

I'm glad I bought all this food. I won't have to shop tomorrow.

| refrigerator | empty | carried | meal |
| grocery store | bought | kitchen | |

Check 1: Did you write sentences that tell the exact words somebody said?

Check 2: Is each sentence punctuated correctly?

★ **Check 3:** Did you tell all the important things that must have happened?

Check 4: Did you indent the first word of each paragraph and begin each paragraph with the right sentence?

Workbook	Passage				★	
	Check 1	Check 2	Check 3	Check 4	Bonus	Total

Lesson 17   **89**

Part A

_____ and _____ were picking apples from a tree.

_____ wore a hat. _____ had a beard. _____ stood on a box. _____ held a bucket. _____ and _____ were sitting on a blanket. _____ read a book.

_____ wore a shirt with the number nine on the back.

_____ drew a picture.

Part B

Instructions: Each sentence begins with a part that tells when. Put in the missing commas.

1. By the time the sun went down we had finished the ice cream and cookies.

2. For seven days nobody said a word.

3. As the boss looked at the empty seats he said, "Business is terrible."

4. At last the rain stopped.

5. After he came in and took a bath Jack said, "I feel great."

6. While everybody else ate dinner in the kitchen Jim stayed in his room and studied.

7. The next day he came to school on time.

Part C

Instructions: The writer forgot to punctuate the sentences that tell the exact words people said. Fix up those sentences.

Kevin and Bill were in the house by themselves. Kevin said I'm bored. Let's play with the football.

Bill said mom told us not to play ball in the house. Kevin didn't listen to Bill. He threw the ball. It went over Bill's head and knocked over the lamp. The lamp fell to the floor and broke. Bill said we're in trouble now. I told you not to throw the ball.

Part D

Instructions: Rewrite the paragraph so that the underlined sentences begin with the part that tells when.

A man wanted to cross the street. He started to walk as soon as the light turned red. He walked quickly. He waved to his friend when he reached the other side of the street.

Part E

Roberto was flying over the ocean when he noticed that his plane was almost out of gas.

Roberto saw a ship in the distance.

| palm trees | smoke | sailed | towed | seaplane | fire |
| built | engine | sputtered | worried | island | tiny |

Check 1: Is each sentence punctuated correctly?

⭐ **Check 2:** Did you tell all the important things that must have happened?

Check 3: Did you indent the first word of each paragraph and begin each paragraph with the right sentence?

Check 4: Did you write sentences that tell the exact words somebody said?

| | Passage | | | | ⭐ | |
Workbook	Check 1	Check 2	Check 3	Check 4	Bonus	Total

Lesson 18   93

Lesson 19

Part A

Instructions: Put the missing comma into each sentence that begins with a part that tells when.

As Wendy drove home from work she thought of the banana pie that was in the refrigerator. Wendy was very hungry because she had not eaten lunch. After she parked her car she ran into the kitchen and opened the refrigerator. Wendy could not believe her eyes. The refrigerator was empty. The banana pie was gone. Everything was gone. While Wendy was looking at the empty refrigerator her brother walked into the kitchen. He looked nervous. After a few seconds he walked up to his sister and said, "I'm sorry. I had some friends over for lunch. We ate all the food. Wait here. I'll be right back." Wendy sat down and waited. After a few minutes her brother walked into the kitchen. He was carrying a bag filled with groceries. While Wendy took a nap her brother cooked dinner. The dessert was a huge banana pie.

Part B

Instructions: The writer forgot to punctuate the sentences that tell the exact words somebody said. Fix up those sentences.

	James did not do his homework last night. He said my teacher won't care. She likes me.
	James was wrong. His teacher did care. She said you will stay in from recess to finish your work.
	James was not happy during recess. He said I will finish my homework tonight before I watch television I don't like missing recess.

Lesson 19   95

Part C

_____ and _____ were playing basketball. _____ bounced a ball. _____ wore shorts and long socks. _____ wore a headband to keep her hair from getting in her eyes. _____ jumped into the air as she shot the ball toward the basket. _____ leaned against a pole as she watched the girls play basketball. _____ read a newspaper. _____ sat on a bench.

Part D

Instructions: Rewrite the paragraph. Begin each underlined sentence with the part that tells when.

    Lisa went fishing yesterday morning. She caught three fish before the sun came up. She made a big meal when she got home. Everybody liked the fresh fish.

Part E

Josh went for a hike in the woods.

That water is cold. I am freezing.

Josh had to dry his clothes.

I think I can start a fire.

broke   wooden bridge   collapsed   stream   soaked   collected
gathered   twigs   magnifying glass   branches   fire   dried

Check 1: Is each sentence punctuated correctly?

★ **Check 2:** Did you tell all the important things that must have happened?

Check 3: Did you indent the first word of each paragraph and begin each paragraph with the right sentence?

Check 4: Did you write sentences that tell the exact words somebody said?

	Passage				★	
Workbook	Check 1	Check 2	Check 3	Check 4	Bonus	Total

Lesson 19   **97**

Lesson 20

Part A

Instructions: Put the missing comma into each sentence that begins with a part that tells when.

Ann went ice-skating on the lake with her little dog. As Ann skated the dog ran behind her. When they were near the middle of the lake Ann saw a hole in the ice. She screamed. The dog tried to stop. It skidded and fell into the hole.

Ann knew she had to act quickly. She skated toward the shore. As she skated she could hear her dog barking. When she reached the shore she grabbed a ladder from a truck. She carried the ladder back to the hole in the ice. She put the ladder next to the hole. The dog put its paws on the end of the ladder. As Ann pulled on the ladder the dog climbed out of the water. Ann picked up the dog and skated to the shore. By the time she reached the shore her dog had started to shiver. Ann took the dog into her car and turned on the heater. After a few minutes the dog stopped shivering and began to wag its tail.

Part B

1. Yolanda put a book on the magazine.

   The book
   It   had a red cover.

2. Ramon got a new coat.

   The coat
   It   had a fur collar.

3. Chang bought a pencil and a pen.

   He gave the pen to his sister.
            it

4. Tom found a dime.

   He gave the dime to his brother.
            it

5. His shoes and his shirt were very dirty.

   His shirt
   It   smelled terrible.

98   Lesson 20

Part C

Instructions: The writer forgot to punctuate the sentences that tell the exact words somebody said. Fix up those sentences.

David walked up to his sister. He said I have a problem. My bike won't work.

She said I will help you fix it. They worked for two hours. After they finished, the bike worked as well as ever.

David said Thanks a lot. I really am happy that you are my sister.

Part D

Instructions: Rewrite this paragraph. Begin each underlined sentence with the part that tells when.

Jamal and Tamicha worked on a car. They fixed the brakes in the morning. They fixed the engine in the afternoon. They painted the car after they ate dinner.

Part E

Mr. Barnes loved to catch fish in Green Lake.

Mr. Barnes was excited.

| fishing | line | pole | snapped | tumbled |
| soaked | caught | shore | row | oars |

Check 1: Is each sentence punctuated correctly?

Check 2: Did you tell all the important things that must have happened?

★ **Check 3:** Did you write sentences that tell the exact words somebody said?

Check 4: Did you use the words *he, she* and *it* so they are clear?

Workbook	Passage				★	
	Check 1	Check 2	Check 3	Check 4	Bonus	Total

Lesson 21

Part A

Instructions: Put the missing comma into each sentence that begins with a part that tells when.

Mr. Ross took his family out for dinner at a fancy restaurant. They had a very expensive meal. After they finished the meal the waiter brought them the bill. Mr. Ross reached into his pocket for his wallet. As he reached into his pocket he realized that he had left his wallet at home. He told the waiter about his problem. The waiter told the boss that Mr. Ross could not pay the bill. When the boss heard about the problem she was not happy. The boss and Mr. Ross talked and came up with a solution to the problem. While his family went home to look for the wallet Mr. Ross had to begin washing dishes. Mr. Ross put on an apron and began to wash the dishes. By the time his family came back with his wallet Mr. Ross had washed all the dishes in the restaurant.

Part B

Instructions: Punctuate these sentences.

1.	Jill asked can I help you
2.	He asked why is the sky blue
3.	The old man said I'll help you fix that
4.	She asked when does the bus leave

Part C

first	soon	sometimes	suddenly	next	finally

1. Suddenly the lights went out.

2. At first nobody could answer the questions.

3. Finally the car started to move up the hill.

4. Just the other day I saw Orlando at the store.

5. Sometimes that part is just one word.

6. One day everybody brought apples to the teacher.

Part D

1. He put the book on the coat.

   The book
   It belonged to his sister.

2. Ann bought a hamburger and an orange drink.

   The hamburger
   It cost a dollar.

3. Julio threw the ball too hard.

   The ball
   It went over the fence.

4. A jet and a helicopter almost crashed last night.

   The helicopter
   It didn't have any lights.

5. We made a pie yesterday.

   The pie
   It tasted great.

6. Rodney dropped the ball and the bat.

   The ball
   It fell on his foot.

Part E

Ana wanted to give her brother a guitar for his birthday.

I don't have enough money.

$400

OPEN

Ana thought of a way to earn money.

SUNGLASS STORE   MUSIC   BAKERY

CAR WASH $5

Thanks a lot. That's the one I wanted.

Ana's brother

| earned | charged | sign | music store | price tag |
| enough | money | present | bought | birthday party |

Check 1: Is each sentence punctuated correctly?

★ **Check 2:** Did you tell all the important things that must have happened?

Check 3: Did you write sentences that tell the exact words somebody said?

Check 4: Did you use the words *he, she* and *it* so they are clear?

	Passage				★	
Workbook	Check 1	Check 2	Check 3	Check 4	Bonus	Total

Lesson 21   **103**

Lesson 22

Part A

Instructions: Put the missing comma into each sentence that begins with a part that tells when.

Buffy was a bear who lived in a park. Buffy and all the other bears liked to eat the food people left in the park. One day Buffy found a jar of pickles. She broke the jar on a rock. She picked up a pickle and ate it. As soon as she tasted it Buffy went crazy. "I love that taste," she said to herself. She chomped pickle after pickle. When they were all gone Buffy had to have some more. She ran into town. She found a hamburger stand. Before anybody knew what was happening Buffy ate all the pickles in the place. Then she left.

As the owner looked at the empty pickle jar he said, "I'm glad that bear is gone." But Buffy came back the next day and did the same thing. For five days the same thing happened. The restaurant owner didn't know what to do. At last he got an idea. He changed the name of the hamburger stand to The Bear Burger Stand. People came from all around to eat at The Bear Burger Stand and watch the bear that ate pickles.

Instructions: Punctuate these sentences.

	1. When Ben got up, he said I'm hungry. What's for breakfast?
	2. As Mary walked down the stairs, she said have you seen my new shoes? I can't find them.
	3. When Tom came into the room, he said what is wrong with Jack? He looks sad.
	4. After the people sat down, the woman said thank you.

Part C

_____ was doing tricks for some girls. _____ held on to a trapeze with its tail while it swung back and forth. _____ held a banana in one hand and used the other hand to tip its hat to the girls. _____ and _____ watched the monkey do tricks. _____ bent down to take a picture. _____ tilted the camera to get the swinging monkey in the picture. _____ stopped skating to watch the monkey. _____ loved the monkey's tricks so much that she laughed and clapped her hands.

Part D

first	soon	sometimes	suddenly	next	finally

1. Finally the bees returned to their nest.

2. At the end of the race everybody was very tired.

3. Suddenly the wind started to blow against our faces.

4. As soon as the rain stopped the girls went outside and continued the game.

5. Sometimes the lions were very friendly.

6. At first the new student didn't say much.

7. On the third day of the trip a young man got sick and had to go home.

8. Soon the bees returned to their hive.

Part E

David told his sister Betty that Toby's birdcage needed to be cleaned.

David wanted to get Betty a new bird.

flew	windowsill	tried	pet store	picture
bought	clapped	cried	newspaper	saleswoman
	opened	chased	excited	

Check 1: Is each sentence punctuated correctly?

★ **Check 2:** Did you tell all the important things that must have happened?

Check 3: Did you use the words *he, she* and *it* so they are clear?

Check 4: Did you write at least one sentence that begins with a part that tells when?

	Passage				★	
Workbook	Check 1	Check 2	Check 3	Check 4	Bonus	Total

Lesson 23

Part A

Instructions: Each sentence begins with a part that tells when. Put in the missing commas.

1. Suddenly the lights went out and the building began to shake.
2. As they entered the room the boss asked, "Where have you been?"
3. The next day he knew all the answers.
4. Finally the buzzer rang and the boxers went back to their corners.
5. Sometimes the boss would let the workers go home an hour early.
6. At the end of the week the teacher said, "You did a great job this week."

Part B

Instructions: Put the missing comma in each sentence that begins with a part that tells when.

After Tim came home from school. He took his dog out to play in the woods. As they played with a Frisbee. They made a lot of noise. Some baby bears heard the noise and came to watch. The mother bear noticed her cubs were missing and ran to find them. When she saw Tim near her babies. She got scared. She ran toward Tim and his dog. As soon as Tim saw the bear. He looked for a tree to climb. By the time the bear reached him. Tim had climbed up the tree with his dog under his arm. The bear left them alone as soon as she saw that her babies were all right.

Part C

In the middle of a class, _____ walked into the room.

_____ walked on its hind legs and carried books like a student.

_____ was busy writing on her clipboard and did not notice the

alligator. _____ sat in the first row. When _____ saw the

alligator, she laughed and clapped her hands. _____ stood to tell the

teacher about the strange new student.

Part D

1. Ana had fun swimming <u>and</u> playing ball and digging in the sand.

2. The girls <u>and</u> boys <u>and</u> dogs and cats slid down the hill.

3. Tyrell read a book <u>and</u> wrote two letters <u>and</u> called his uncle and cleaned his room.

4. A cat <u>and</u> a dog <u>and</u> a pig and a horse ran into the barn.

Part E

The telephone rang while
Andy was ironing clothes.

Andy

Jason was hanging a picture on the wall upstairs.

Where is the smoke coming from?

Jason

telephone	next	room	smoke	fire extinguisher
sprayed	stairs	worried	clothes basket	
through	doorway	downstairs	ironing board	

Check 1: Is each sentence punctuated correctly?

Check 2: Did you tell all the important things that must have happened?

Check 3: Did you use the words *he, she* and *it* so they are clear?

★ **Check 4:** Did you write at least two sentences that begin with a part that tells when?

	Passage				★	
Workbook	Check 1	Check 2	Check 3	Check 4	Bonus	Total

Lesson 23 **111**

Lesson 24

Part A

Instructions: Each sentence begins with a part that tells when. Put in the missing commas.

1. As the girls walked into the room Mrs. Jones said, "Where have you been?"

2. When the game ended Pablo walked up to the coach and said, "Thank you for teaching us so much. We couldn't have won without your help."

3. When the movie began someone said, "Please turn on the heat."

4. After the teacher finished marking the tests he said, "You are a great group of students."

5. As Ricky walked toward the door he said, "I'm sorry for being so late."

Part B

Instructions: Put the missing comma in each sentence that begins with a part that tells when.

While Jeannie was on her way to school one morning. She found a small black pen. Jeannie picked up the pen and put it into her pocket. When Jeannie got to school. She took the pen out and started writing with it. She was very surprised when she looked at what she had written. The ink in the pen was many different colors. As Jeannie looked at her writing. She thought the colors were the most beautiful colors in the world. Jeannie showed her best friend the wonderful pen. Soon. All of the children were crowding each other to get a look at the pen. After a few minutes. The teacher walked over. He told Jeannie that she was very lucky to have found such a wonderful pen.

Part C

_____ and _____ were clowns. _____ entertained the kids by walking on a tightrope. _____ held out his arms to balance himself and looked straight ahead so he wouldn't fall. _____ sat on Bob's shoulder. _____ tipped its hat to the children as Bob did his act. _____ walked on his hands in front of the clapping kids. The kids laughed at the _____ that sat on Tom's head.

Part D

1.	"Today is my birthday," she said.
2.	We won the game by two points he shouted
3.	I rode my bike to school Mary answered
4.	That is my dog he said
5.	His arm is not broken the doctor whispered
6.	I am hungry the boy said

Part E

Instructions: Fix up each sentence so the word *and* appears only one time.

1. Gwen <u>and</u> Tim <u>and</u> Ebony and Jose played basketball.

2. Angela fixed the brakes <u>and</u> put oil into the engine and waxed the fenders.

3. A book <u>and</u> a pencil <u>and</u> a cup and four plates fell off the table.

Part F

Mrs. Johnson was washing the dishes when she heard a funny noise outside.

Can you help me? I don't feel very well.

Mrs. Johnson

space creature

Mrs. Johnson took the creature into the house.

This chicken soup will make you feel better.

spaceship	model	stomach	drooping	thermometer
blanket	creature	antennas	strange	
prepared	kettle	after a while		

Check 1: Is each sentence punctuated correctly?

Check 2: Did you tell all the important things that must have happened?

Check 3: Did you use the words *he, she* and *it* so they are clear?

★ **Check 4:** Did you write at least two sentences that begin with a part that tells when?

	Passage				★	
Workbook	Check 1	Check 2	Check 3	Check 4	Bonus	Total

Lesson 24   115

Part A

1.	"The sun is shining," Lee shouted.
2.	The plane will land in ten minutes the pilot said
3.	I bought a new shirt at the store he said
4.	This story is very funny the boy thought

Part B

Instructions: Put the missing comma in each sentence that begins with a part that tells when.

Mr. Jones was driving home from the lake with his daughter Nancy and her pet dog. As they were about to cross a bridge. Mr. Jones noticed that the bridge had a big hole in it. He stopped the car and got out to see if the bridge was safe. When Mr. Jones opened the car door. The dog jumped out of the car and started to chase a bird. The dog fell through the hole and landed in the water.

While Mr. Jones ran to the car Nancy watched the dog. In a few moments. Mr. Jones came back with a rope. He tied one end of the rope to the railing on the bridge and threw the other end into the water. As Mr. Jones watched. Nancy climbed down the rope. She grabbed the dog and climbed carefully back up to the bridge. Later that night. Mr. Jones told everyone how brave Nancy had been.

Part C

1. Marcus went to the park with Mike.

   A car splashed water on Marcus.
                           him.

2. Ana and Susan ran down the street.

   A cat ran in front of Susan.
                          her.

3. Tim saw Susan on the bus.

   The bus driver was giving Susan change.
                              her

4. Rodney talked to Jeff.

   Everybody liked Rodney.
                    him.

5. Alberto and Jerome went to the movies.

   The grocer had given Jerome four dollars for cleaning the snow
                         him

   off the street.

Part D

1. Kim got into the car and turned on the engine and drove home.

2. Mary and Latrell and Tim and Amanda were sick yesterday.

3. Oscar wore black shoes and a white shirt and brown pants and a red tie.

Part E

Julia watched as Tina tried to ride a wild horse.

corral	fence	bucked	lasso	chased	galloped
threw	neck	stopped	brought	suddenly	

Check 1: Is each sentence punctuated correctly?

★ **Check 2:** Did you tell all the important things that must have happened?

Check 3: Did you use the words *he, she* and *it* so they are clear?

Check 4: Did you write at least two sentences that begin with a part that tells when?

	Passage				★	
Workbook	Check 1	Check 2	Check 3	Check 4	Bonus	Total

Part A

Instructions: Put the missing commas in each sentence that begins with a part that tells when.

Maria had a pet bird that she loved very much. One day. Maria noticed that its birdcage was dirty. She got some supplies and began to clean the cage. While she was cleaning the cage. the bird flew out the open cage door. Maria could not catch the bird and started to cry. When Maria's father heard her crying. He came into the room and tried to catch the bird with a net. The bird flew out the open window.

After her bird flew away. Maria was very sad. Her father did not know what to do. Finally. Her father went to the pet store to buy a bird for Maria. The pet store had several birds that looked just like Maria's bird. Her father bought one of them and brought it home. When Maria got up the next morning. She clapped her hands and smiled. A beautiful bird was sitting on a swing in the birdcage.

Part B

1.	"Where are my books? she asked.
2.	"How old is the car he asked
3.	Did you like it Tom asked
4.	I didn't like it at all Tyrell thought to himself
5.	We got home early he said
6.	Was he late she asked

Part C

1. Tim helped Robert clean the yard.

   A woman gave Robert five dollars.
                   him

2. Tim waved at Susan.

   Everybody knew Susan.
                  her.

3. My mom called my brother.

   She asked my brother why the bus was so late.
             him

4. We saw Tim and Robert in the park.

   We didn't know that Mrs. Jones was looking for Robert.
                                                   him.

5. Ellen walked to school with Anita.

   Everybody liked Anita.
                 her.

Part D

Instructions: Write each sentence so the word *and* appears only once.

1. The boy ran and slipped on the ice and fell down.

2. John and Ana and Kevin and their dogs went jogging.

3. They were tired and thirsty and hungry and dirty.

Part E

Serena and Melissa were playing baseball in an empty lot.

| baseball | broke | Jeep | drove | bought | fixed |
| putty | window pane | accidentally | terrible | relieved |

Check 1: Is each sentence punctuated correctly?

★ **Check 2:** Did you tell all the important things that must have happened?

Check 3: Did you use the words *he, she* and *it* so they are clear?

Check 4: Did you write at least two sentences that begin with a part that tells when?

Workbook	Passage				★	
	Check 1	Check 2	Check 3	Check 4	Bonus	Total

Lesson 26   121

Part A

Instructions: Put the missing comma in each sentence that begins with a part that tells when.

A baker had just finished baking a cherry pie. A fly smelled the fresh pie and flew toward an open window in the bakery. While the baker put whipped cream on top of the pie. The fly entered the bakery through the open window. The baker saw the fly and got a flyswatter. When the fly landed near the pie. The baker swung the flyswatter at the fly. The baker missed the fly. The flyswatter landed in the pie. When the flyswatter hit the pie. The pie splattered all over the baker. As the baker wiped the pie off her face the fly flew out the window. Before she started baking another pie the baker made sure that all the windows were closed.

Part B

1.	"Where are my gloves? he asked.
2.	"What is that she asked
3.	Did you go to the movies last night Tony asked
4.	We stayed home last night Jim answered
5.	I saw a funny movie she said
6.	How old are you today he asked

Part C

1. Randy went to the show with Vanessa.

   Randy / He liked rock and roll music.

2. Jerry bought an apple and an orange.

   The apple / It cost 75 cents.

3. Amanda waved to her brother.

   Amanda / She had just won the race.

4. Lisa and Susan waited for the bus.

   A boy began to talk to Lisa. / her.

5. Tom and Mike walked to school.

   A car splashed water on Tom. / him.

Lesson 27   **123**

Part D

1. Make up a sentence that tells the four things that were in the back of the pickup truck. Start your sentence by naming those things.

   ███████████████████ *were in the back of the pickup truck.*

2. Make up a sentence that tells the three things that waited in line at the drive-up window. Start your sentence by naming those things.

   ███████████████████ *waited in line at the drive-up window.*

3. Make up a sentence that tells the four things that were on sale. Start your sentence by naming those things.

   ███████████████████ *were on sale.*

bathtub	desk	chair	van
motorcycle	tire	pickup truck	

Part E

Bob talked to the zookeeper while his sister Leslie went to look at the bears.

bear	elephant's trunk	cage	climbed	knew
fixed	fence	broke	tumbled	
leaned	lifted	terrified		

Check 1: Is each sentence punctuated correctly?

⋆ **Check 2:** Did you tell all the important things that must have happened?

Check 3: Did you use the words *he, she* and *it* so they are clear?

Check 4: Did you write at least two sentences that begin with a part that tells when?

	Passage				⋆	
Workbook	Check 1	Check 2	Check 3	Check 4	Bonus	Total

Lesson 27   **125**

Part A

①

Ann went ice-skating with Jane and Mary. As they were skating, Ann said, "Let's have a race to the other side of the lake."

Mary said, "That's a great idea. Let's go." The girls skated as quickly as they could.

As they were skating, Jane said, "I am the greatest. I will win this race."

"Oh no, you won't," Ann shouted. Jane and Ann argued about who would win the race. While they argued, Mary skated as fast as she could. Mary won the race easily.

Mary said, "If you two had spent less time arguing, one of you might have won the race."

"I learned a good lesson," Ann said, as she shook hands with Jane.

②

Ann went ice-skating with Jane and Mary. As they were skating, Ann said, "Let's have a race to the other side of the lake." Mary said, "That's a great idea. Let's go." The girls skated as quickly as they could. As they were skating, Jane said, "I am the greatest. I will win this race." "Oh no, you won't," Ann shouted. Jane and Ann argued about who would win the race. While they argued, Mary skated as fast as she could. Mary won the race easily. Mary said, "If you two had spent less time arguing, one of you might have won the race." "I learned a good lesson," Ann said, as she shook hands with Jane.

Part B

1.	Are you feeling well he asked
2.	Did you stay out late last night his mom asked
3.	I got home early he said
4.	We ran four miles Ana yelled
5.	Did you find the shirt you were looking for she asked

Part C

1. The boys and the girls were working in the yard.

   The girls
   They raked the leaves.

2. The horses jumped over the fence.

   The horses
   They headed toward the grassy field.

3. The boys chased the birds.

   The birds
   They made a lot of noise.

4. Mrs. Lopez spoke to the boys.

   She told the boys them where to find the bus stop.

5. The girls got ready for the game.

   The girls
   They were nervous.

6. Tyrell put the forks and knives on the table.

   He put the forks them on the left side of each plate.

Part D

cake
watermelon
chicken

1. Make up a sentence that tells the three animals that ate dinner. Start your sentence by naming those animals.

   ████████████████████ *ate dinner.*

2. Make up a sentence that tells the three things that the animals ate. Start your sentence this way: *The animals ate.*

3. Make up a sentence that tells the four things that the bear wore. Start your sentence this way: *The bear wore.*

tie	glasses	gloves	tiger	monkey	bear

Part E

James and Marcus wanted to get some fresh honey.

I think you are making a big mistake. Let's just go to the store and buy some honey.

Beehive

Marcus

James

Those bees are angry.

James

| swarmed | ladder | reached | breathed | ignored |
| pond | pickup truck | remained | chased |

Check 1: Is each sentence punctuated correctly?

★ **Check 2:** Did you tell all the important things that must have happened?

Check 3: Did you write at least two sentences that begin with a part that tells when?

Check 4: Are there any unclear words in your paragraphs?

	Passage				★	
Workbook	Check 1	Check 2	Check 3	Check 4	Bonus	Total

Lesson 29

Part A

1. Antonio bought two pencils and four pens.

   He gave the pencils   to his friend.
            them

2. Kenyon found three bottles on the beach.

   He put the bottles   in a garbage can.
           them

3. We saw lions and tigers at the zoo.

   The tigers   had stripes on their bodies.
   They

4. Two men and three boys went for a drive.

   The boys   sat in the backseat.
   They

5. The girls were climbing up the mountain.

   The girls   were almost at the top.
   They

Part B

Instructions: The writer forgot to punctuate the sentences that tell the exact words somebody said. Fix up those sentences.

Kevin loved to tell jokes. One day, he walked up to his brother and said can I ask you a question

You sure can his brother said

Why did the chicken cross the road Kevin asked

I don't know his brother said

The chicken crossed the road to get to the other side Kevin said Kevin laughed and laughed. He loved that joke.

Lesson 29 **131**

Part C

①

Mr. Smith stopped at a restaurant to get a cup of coffee. He walked up to the counter and said, "I'll have a cup of that delicious coffee." After he finished the coffee, he discovered that he had no money in his pocket. He walked up to the cashier and said, "I forgot my money."

"You owe us two dollars for the coffee," the cashier said. The boss heard Mr. Smith talking to the cashier.

The boss said, "You will have to wash dishes if you don't pay your bill."

"Show me where the kitchen is," Mr. Smith said. Mr. Smith was not happy. Just when Mr. Smith was about to walk into the kitchen, his son ran into the restaurant.

His son said, "You forgot your wallet this morning. Here it is."

"Thank goodness," Mr. Smith said as he paid for his coffee. Then Mr. Smith bought his son a big cup of hot chocolate.

"Thanks for buying me the hot chocolate," his son said.

Mr. Smith said, "I'm glad you found the wallet. I don't like washing dishes."

②

Mr. Smith stopped at a restaurant to get a cup of coffee. He walked up to the counter and said, "I'll have a cup of that delicious coffee." After he finished the coffee, he discovered that he had no money in his pocket. He walked up to the cashier and said, "I forgot my money." "You owe us two dollars for the coffee," the cashier said. The boss heard Mr. Smith talking to the cashier. The boss said, "You will have to wash dishes if you don't pay your bill." "Show me where the kitchen is," Mr. Smith said. Mr. Smith was not happy. Just when Mr. Smith was about to walk into the kitchen, his son ran into the restaurant. His son said, "You forgot your wallet this morning. Here it is." "Thank goodness," Mr. Smith said as he paid for his coffee. Then Mr. Smith bought his son a big cup of hot chocolate. "Thanks for buying me the hot chocolate," his son said. Mr. Smith said, "I'm glad you found the wallet. I don't like washing dishes."

132   Lesson 29

Part D

1. Make up a sentence that tells the three things that the animals ate. Start your sentence this way: *The animals ate.*

2. Make up a sentence that tells the three kinds of animals that lived in the barn. Start your sentence by naming those animals.
   [redacted] *lived in the barn.*

3. Make up a sentence that tells the four things that were hanging on the wall. Start your sentence by naming those things.
   [redacted] *were hanging on the wall.*

an ax	saw	hammer	shovel

Part E

After James finished cooking a fancy dinner for his date, he went upstairs to change clothes.

| restaurant | ruined | chicken | salad | flowers |
| | bought | tablecloth | vase | |

Check 1: Is each sentence punctuated correctly?

★ **Check 2:** Did you tell all the important things that must have happened?

Check 3: Are there any unclear words in your paragraphs?

Check 4: Did you write at least two sentences that begin with a part that tells when?

Workbook	Passage				★	
	Check 1	Check 2	Check 3	Check 4	Bonus	Total

Test 2

Part A

Instructions: Put a comma in each sentence that begins with a part that tells when.

Mrs. James told her husband that there was going to be an art contest. Mr. James loved to paint pictures. When he heard about the art contest he got out his painting materials and began work on a picture. After he worked on the painting for two days. The painting was almost finished. Mr. James stepped back to look at his picture. As he stepped back. He heard a loud noise. He saw their dog chasing their cat across the floor. The cat bumped into the easel. The easel tipped over. The painting and bottles of paint flew into the air. As the painting fell to the ground paint from the open bottles splattered over the painting. Mr. James was very upset. He left the room to take a walk. Mrs. James heard the noise. When she walked into the room she saw the painting. She thought that the painting was wonderful. She sent the painting to the art contest. Seven days later Mr. James received a letter telling him that his picture had won the contest.

Part B

Instructions: The writer forgot to punctuate the sentences that tell the exact words somebody said. Fix up those sentences.

1.	We won the game by two points he shouted
2.	I rode my bike to school Mary answered
3.	Is that your dog he asked
4.	His arm is not broken the doctor whispered

Part C

1. Gary went to the show with Alice.

   $\begin{array}{l}\text{Alice} \\ \text{She}\end{array}$ fell asleep during the movie.

2. Antonio bought a new shirt and a new jacket.

   $\begin{array}{l}\text{The jacket} \\ \text{It}\end{array}$ was made of wool.

3. Tom and Kevin ran in the race.

   Nobody has ever beaten $\begin{array}{l}\text{Kevin} \\ \text{him}\end{array}$ in a race.

4. Mary and Robert helped fix the car.

   $\begin{array}{l}\text{Mary} \\ \text{She}\end{array}$ worked on the engine.

5. We sent a present to our sister and our grandmother.

   The present took two weeks to get to $\begin{array}{l}\text{our sister} \\ \text{her}\end{array}$.

Part D

Instructions: Rewrite each sentence so that it has only one *and*.

1. Jerry juggled a baseball and a basketball and a volleyball and a football.

2. Jason and Thomas and Mary and Lee scored 95 on the math test.

3. Mrs. Lee climbed up the stairs and opened the door and walked into the apartment.

Part E

Roger had just captured a valuable monkey.

The baby monkey had a plan to rescue its mother.

hammock	asleep	unlocked	opened
	cage	key	banana

Check 1: Is each sentence punctuated correctly?

Check 2: Did you tell all the important things that must have happened?

Check 3: Did you use the words *he, she* and *it* so they are clear?

Check 4: Did you write at least two sentences that begin with a part that tells when?

	Passage				★	
Workbook	Check 1	Check 2	Check 3	Check 4	Bonus	Total

Lesson 31

Part A

Instructions: Each sentence begins with a part that tells when. Put in the missing commas.

1. As we walked home Michael said, "I liked that movie."
2. When the alarm clock rang John jumped out of bed and asked, "What are we having for breakfast?"
3. After we finished supper I walked over to Dad and said, "Those hamburgers tasted wonderful."
4. As Vanessa walked up the stairs she said, "I'm going to finish my science homework."
5. Before she walked onto the stage she said, "I feel great. I'm going to sing for three hours."

Part B

Instructions: The writer forgot to punctuate the sentences that tell the exact words somebody said. Fix up those sentences.

Lisa was about to make her first parachute jump. As she looked at the ground far below, she wasn't sure she wanted to jump. I'm nervous she said to the pilot.

Everybody is nervous the first time they make a parachute jump the pilot said. The pilot smiled at Lisa.

I feel better now Lisa said. She looked out the door of the plane. After a few seconds, she jumped into the air. As she jumped, her parachute opened. This is great Lisa said to herself.

Part C

Instructions: Write the letter *P* in front of each sentence that should start a new paragraph.

One day, a hunter caught a rabbit in the woods. The hunter grabbed the rabbit by the ears and said, "I am going to cook you for dinner." The rabbit kicked and squirmed, but it could not get away. The hunter said, "Soon, I will have a fine rabbit dinner." "Please, please, Mr. Hunter, let me go!" the rabbit begged. The hunter laughed. "Why should I let you go?" the hunter asked.

The rabbit thought fast. Soon, a sneaky smile spread across its face. It said, "If you don't let me go, I can't show you where the buried treasure is." "What is this buried treasure?" the hunter shouted, shaking the rabbit by its long ears. The rabbit said, "It is a very wonderful treasure. If you will just put me down for a few seconds, I will go get it for you." "All right," the hunter said.

The greedy hunter put the rabbit down and clapped his hands with joy at the thought of the buried treasure. He waited and waited for the rabbit to come back. After an hour, he said, "I wonder if that rabbit tricked me."

The rabbit never came back. It ran into the hole in the ground where its family lived. As the rabbit hopped into the hole, it said, "I tricked another hunter. That buried treasure trick works every time!" "You mustn't play with hunters anymore," the mother rabbit said as she gave her son a big hug.

Part D

1. Make up a sentence that tells four things the juggler balanced. Start your sentence this way: *The juggler balanced.*

2. Make up a sentence that tells what Tom sold. Start your sentence this way: *Tom sold.*

3. Make up a sentence that tells the four animals that walked across the tightrope. Start your sentence by naming those animals.

   ▆▆▆▆▆▆▆▆▆▆▆▆▆▆▆ *walking across the tight rope.*

bear	cat	drinks	popcorn	candy	ball
chair	bottle	seal	lamp	monkey	

Lesson 31   **141**

Part E

Instructions: Write two paragraphs that tell what happened.

Gary took Rover for a walk in the woods.

I hurt my ankle. Go get help.

Rover

Gary

Come back with my glove.

Rhonda   Maria   Lois

Lois   Maria   Rhonda

| chased | hole | stepped | splint | baseball glove |
| stole | painful | field | tied | sprained |

Check 1: Is each sentence punctuated correctly?

★ **Check 2:** Did you tell all the important things that must have happened?

Check 3: Are there any unclear words in your paragraphs?

Check 4: Did you write at least one sentence that names three or four things?

	Passage				★	
Workbook	Check 1	Check 2	Check 3	Check 4	Bonus	Total

Lesson 32

Part A

Instructions: Put the letter *P* in front of each sentence that should start a new paragraph.

A baby bear was running through the forest when it smelled honey. It looked up and saw a beehive. As it ran home to tell its parents what it had found, the baby bear said, "I love fresh honey." When the baby bear got home, it said, "I found a beehive full of honey!" "That's wonderful," the father bear said.

The mother bear and father bear followed the baby bear to the beehive. "How can we get at the honey without getting stung by the bees?" the mother bear said as she looked hungrily at the beehive. The father bear said, "I'll get the bees mad at me. When they fly out after me, you two can get the honey." "That's a great idea," the baby bear said.

The father bear smeared himself with mud so that the bees could not sting him. Then he ran around the beehive. No bees came out. The mother bear whispered, "Be careful, dear." "Watch this," the father bear said. He hit the beehive with his paw. The bees came out of the hive. The father bear started to run. "Quick, mama, let's get the honey!" the baby bear shouted. As the mother bear and baby bear got the honey, they heard a loud scream. "Ouch, ouch! I forgot to smear mud on my rear!" the father bear yelled. The bear family enjoyed the honey very much, but one of the bears had to stand up while he ate.

Part B

Instructions: Fix up the four unclear words in this passage.

One day, Tom and his dog went to the park with a Frisbee. The dog loved to play with the Frisbee and wagged its tail as they went to the park. As Tom and his dog played, they came out of the woods to watch.

Tom was pretending he was a star baseball player. He threw the Frisbee as hard as he could. It went over the dog's head and landed in the field. Tom and his dog ran after the Frisbee. It chewed the Frisbee.

As the dog barked at the bear cubs, she came out from behind the trees. When Tom saw the mother bear, he grabbed it and climbed up a tree.

Part C

Instructions: The writer forgot to punctuate sentences that tell the exact words somebody said. Fix up those sentences.

Late one night, Ellen was watching television with her friend Susan. Suddenly, they heard a loud boom. What was that Ellen said.

Susan said I don't know. Maybe it was an accident. The two girls ran out to the sidewalk to see what had happened. They looked but did not see anything. As they were walking along, they began to hear a humming noise.

Look at those strange flashing lights over there Ellen said. Cautiously, the girls walked toward the lights. As they got closer to where the noise was coming from, they heard another sound. It sounded like someone moaning with pain. It must have been an accident Ellen whispered.

It sounds like somebody's hurt Susan said.

The noise and lights seemed to come from around the corner. The girls turned the corner and stopped in their tracks. In front of them was a huge metal disk that looked like a spaceship. It had crashed in the middle of Elm Street. Near the disk, a strange creature was sitting on the ground. He turned to the girls and said I come from the planet Mars. You must help me.

Part D

1. They will be sad if they lose the game.
2. He will go with us unless he is sick.
3. She won the race although she had a bad cold.

Part E

Jerome, David and Mario were playing football in the park near Jerome's house.

boards   hammer   paintbrush   rag   kicked   knocked

bird's nest   built   painted   carried   garage

Check 1: Is each sentence punctuated correctly?

Check 2: Did you tell all the important things that must have happened?

Check 3: Are there any unclear words in your paragraphs?

★ **Check 4:** Did you write at least one sentence that names three or four things?

	Passage				★	
Workbook	Check 1	Check 2	Check 3	Check 4	Bonus	Total

146   Lesson 32

Lesson 33

Part A

Instructions: Put the letter *P* in front of each sentence that should start a new paragraph.

Tim prepared to make his first parachute jump. As Tim looked out the door of the plane, he said, "It sure is a long way down to the ground." Then Tim looked at his instructor and said, "I don't think I can jump." "You can do it," the instructor said. As Tim looked down, he replied, "But I sure am scared." "Just close your eyes, count to 10 and jump," the instructor said.

Tim did what his instructor told him to do. He forced himself to take a deep breath and count to 10. Then he jumped. A few moments later, Tim felt a great tug as his parachute opened. As Tim floated down, he said, "This is fun." "Good job," the instructor said to himself as he watched from the plane.

Part B

1. "I'll be glad to help you," she said. "I'm not doing anything right now."

2. Thank you very much the lion said to the mouse. I'll never forget what you have done.

3. I don't feel well Jim said to his mother. My head hurts.

4. I hope she sits next to me Mike whispered. She is very smart.

5. That is not my hat Adam said to the teacher. My hat has red and gold stripes.

Part C

Instructions: Fix up the four unclear words.

Ramon and Kevin worked at a rodeo. Kevin was a cowboy who rode bulls. He was a rodeo clown who helped cowboys.

One day, he tried to ride a fierce bull. He held on tightly as the bull jumped up and down. Suddenly, the bull turned sharply and threw Kevin to the ground. As Kevin sat on the ground holding his leg, he ran into the rodeo arena holding it over his head. Ramon put the barrel down on the ground and began to yell at the bull. The bull turned and ran toward the barrel. While Ramon helped Kevin walk away, the bull hit the barrel with its horns. Ramon had once again helped a cowboy who was in danger.

Part D

Instructions: Write each sentence so it begins with the part that can be moved.

1. We will be very happy if we win the game.
2. She will win the race unless she falls down.
3. The field was dry although it rained all night.

Part E

After school, David took his dogs for a walk.

Come back here. Keep away from those skunks.

Setter

Poodle Collie

Beagle

What an awful stink.

path	tripped	baby skunk	awful
	scrubbed	terrible	

Check 1: Is each sentence punctuated correctly?

Check 2: Did you tell all the important things that must have happened?

Check 3: Are there any unclear words in your paragraphs?

★ **Check 4:** Did you write at least one sentence that names three or four things?

	Passage				★	
Workbook	Check 1	Check 2	Check 3	Check 4	Bonus	Total

Lesson 34

Part A

1. "Are you sick?" his mom asked. "You look pale."

2. I'm not feeling well Jason said to his mom. Can we go home now

3. Where is the bus station Jerry asked. I want to go to New York

4. The train is late the conductor announced. It will not be here for 20 minutes

5. What time is it Alberto asked his friend. We have to be home by six o'clock

Part B

Instructions: Fix up the three unclear words in this passage.

Raymond loved to throw rocks. While Raymond was walking through the woods one day, he picked up some rocks and started throwing them at a tree. One rock missed the tree and hit it. They were very mad. They flew out of the hive and headed straight toward Raymond. He ran away as quickly as he could. Just before the bees reached Raymond, he jumped into it. He stayed in the pond until the bees returned to their nest.

Part C

Instructions: Put the letter *P* in front of each sentence that should start a new paragraph.

A king could not find his favorite bracelet. The king said, "I would give anything to find that bracelet." The king looked all around his kingdom for the bracelet. Finally, he came to a crow. The king asked the crow, "Have you seen my favorite bracelet?" "Yes, I have," the crow said. The king said, "Will you help me get the bracelet?" "I will get the bracelet for you if you do something for me," the crow said. The king wanted his bracelet back. He said to the crow, "Just tell me what you want. I will give anything to you if you get me the bracelet." The crow said, "I would like a pound of birdseed to eat every day." "You shall have it!" the king said. The crow flew off to get the king's bracelet. When the crow returned with the bracelet, the king gave the crow a pound of birdseed. The king was happy because he got back his bracelet. The crow was happy because it had a lot to eat.

Part D

Instructions: Write each sentence so it begins with the part that can be moved.

1. She went to the show although she was not feeling well.
2. We will go swimming unless it rains.
3. He will get sick if he keeps on eating so much.

Part E

The pirates captured the ship.

The captain

If you want to live, tell us where the treasure is.

Pegleg

Redbeard

Snake Eye

the cabin boy

The treasure is in this chest.

| plank | pirates | captured | tripped |
| dagger | rope | congratulated | attention |

Check 1: Is each sentence punctuated correctly?

★ **Check 2:** Did you tell all the important things that must have happened?

Check 3: Are there any unclear words in your paragraphs?

Check 4: Did you write at least one sentence that names three or four things?

| | Passage | | | | ★ | |
Workbook	Check 1	Check 2	Check 3	Check 4	Bonus	Total

Part A

1. The car was old. It was in good condition.
   The car was old, but it was in good condition.

2. John tried to lift up the car but it was too heavy.

3. He wanted to go to the movies but he did not have enough money.

4. We put a fence around the yard but the deer were still able to get to the garden.

5. Tom was tired but he ran very fast.

Part B

Instructions: Put the letter *P* in front of each sentence that should start a new paragraph.

A mouse was running away from a cat as fast as it could. As the mouse ran, it yelled, "Help, help!" The cat was getting closer and closer. There was nowhere for the poor mouse to hide. The only thing in sight was a big turtle. "Mr. Turtle, please save me from this cat!" the mouse shouted. "You can crawl inside my shell," the turtle said. "The cat can't hurt you in there." So the mouse jumped into the turtle's shell.

When the cat reached the turtle, the turtle pulled in its head and legs. The cat was angry. "I know where you are, you silly mouse," the cat said. The cat ran all around the turtle trying to find a way to get at the mouse, but it could not find a way in. After a long while, the turtle said, "It sounds like the cat is gone." He poked out his head. The cat was nowhere to be seen. "Thanks very much for saving me from the cat," said the mouse as it crawled out of the shell. "It was a pleasure," the turtle said. "I enjoyed fooling the cat."

Part C

Instructions: In each item, a person says two things. Put in the missing punctuation marks.

1. Can I stay up late Tim asked his mother. I have a lot of homework to do

2. Stay back the policeman said to the children. That tree looks like it's going to fall

3. I will try he said softly. I promise

4. My puppy is lost the boy said. Can you help me find it

Part D

Instructions: Write each sentence so that it begins with the part that tells where.

1. The road got bumpy near the river.

2. Two ducks were eating in front of my house.

3. The clouds were darker above the mountain peak.

Part E

Susie and Alex were getting ready to cook dinner when they heard a loud noise inside the cave.

| stretched | stood | away | scared | roared | furry |

Check 1: Is each sentence punctuated correctly?
Check 2: Did you begin at least one sentence with a part that tells when?
Check 3: Are there any unclear words in your paragraphs?
★ **Check 4:** Did you start a new paragraph when another person started talking?

	Passage				★	
Workbook	Check 1	Check 2	Check 3	Check 4	Bonus	Total

Lesson 35   **155**

Lesson 36

Part A

1. Anita wanted to go to the show but all the tickets had been sold.
2. David went to bed early but he did not fall asleep until midnight.
3. Rosa made 10 dollars washing cars but she still didn't have enough money to buy the guitar she wanted.
4. We wanted to go swimming but the water was too cold.
5. They tried to call home but the line was busy.

Part B

Instructions: Fix up the three unclear words in this passage.

Early one morning, Tina drove her car to the garage where Robert, Sam and

Jane worked. After Tina parked her car in front of the gas pumps, he walked to

the back of the car and opened the gas tank cover. As Robert put gas in the car,

he cleaned the front windows. She bent down and took a tire off a car while the

men worked on Tina's car.

Part C

1. They will come with us unless it rains.
2. Although the sky was cloudy we decided to go to the beach.
3. The girls talked a lot as they prepared for the picnic.
4. If Marcus gets this word right he will be the class spelling champion.
5. Unless the other team scores five points our team will win the game.
6. The little horse jumped up when it saw the carrot.
7. We will be late if the bus doesn't come soon.
8. If you see my brother tell him to be home by eight o'clock.

Part D

Instructions: In each item, a person says two things. Put in the missing punctuation marks.

1.	Can I stay up late Tony asked his mother. My favorite show is on television
2.	Where have you been the teacher said to Josh. The class started 10 minutes ago
3.	I am not feeling well Tom said to his mom. Can we go home now
4.	I will win Serena said. I am the greatest

Part E

Instructions: Write each sentence so it begins with the part that tells where.

1. Two boys were eating in the big room.

2. My friends were playing cards on the porch.

3. The water was very cold near the rocks.

Part F

Mike and James looked at the robot they had just assembled.

wrecked   haywire   fishbowl   scared   television   overturned

Check 1: Is each sentence punctuated correctly?

Check 2: Did you begin at least one sentence with a part that tells when?

Check 3: Are there any unclear words in your paragraphs?

★ **Check 4:** Did you start a new paragraph when another speaker started talking?

Workbook	Passage				★	
	Check 1	Check 2	Check 3	Check 4	Bonus	Total

Part A

Instructions: Fix up the three unclear words in this passage.

Tom

Ricky

the creature

Tom

Ricky

Tom and Ricky were picking apples when they heard a strange noise. The boys looked up and saw a funny-looking creature walking toward them. The boys were scared. When the creature waved its arm, he fell off a tree branch. He turned around and started to run away. The creature caught him and put him gently on the ground.

Part B

1. The man played the piano after he read the newspaper.
2. If she is late she will miss the bus.
3. Near the edge of the river the road got bumpy.
4. Although Tyrell was sick he went to school.
5. My best friend was tired after the race.
6. By the end of the summer we had collected 200 seashells.
7. The little deer lifted its head when it heard a noise.

Part C

One day, a rock hit a fishbowl. The rock hit the fishbowl very hard and made a big crack in the bowl. The water in the fishbowl began to drip out of the crack. It was not dripping very fast but the fish knew that all the water would drip out of their tank within a day. The fish were worried. If all the water dripped out of their tank, they would die. The water in the bowl got lower and lower.

The only way to stop the water from dripping out was to seal the crack. The fish tried filling the crack with sand from the bottom of the fishbowl but the grains of sand were too big to fit into the crack. The fish couldn't seal the crack with sand. A fish put its fin over the crack to hold the water inside the tank but the water went around the fish fin and dripped out of the crack. Finally, a fish pulled snails from the side of the tank and stuck them over the crack. The snails were sticky. They sealed the tank so that no more water could drip out. The fish did not have to worry about the crack anymore.

Part D

Instructions: In each item, a person says two things. Put in the missing punctuation marks.

1. Why are you so happy his dad asked. Did your team win the game

2. I need help with my homework Tim said to Maria. Will you help me with my math

3. Stay back Kim shouted. I saw a big snake on the path

4. Why is everybody clapping David asked his friends. Is the movie over

Part E

Just after the school bell rang, a strange thing happened.

carrying   surprised   startled   clipboard   interesting   attendance

Check 1: Is each sentence punctuated correctly?

Check 2: Did you begin at least one sentence with a part that tells when?

Check 3: Are there any unclear words in your paragraphs?

★ **Check 4:** Did you start a new paragraph when another speaker started talking?

	Passage				★	
Workbook	Check 1	Check 2	Check 3	Check 4	Bonus	Total

Lesson 37   **161**

Lesson 38

Part A

Instructions: Four sentences need commas because they begin with a part that tells when, where, *if, although* or *unless.* Put in the missing commas.

1. I got home before the rain started.
2. If we win this game we will be the champs.
3. His mom will take him to the movies if he gets an A on the test.
4. Under the front porch a cat was taking care of its kittens.
5. If the movie ends after midnight we will have to walk home.
6. Although she was sick she went to the party.
7. My friend missed three days of school last week.

Part B

Instructions: Punctuate the sentences that tell the exact words somebody said.

As Jessica ran into the room, she threw up her arms and yelled our team won the game. We are the champs.

That is wonderful, Jessica's mother said. What was the score?

We scored five runs. The other team scored two runs Jessica said. I hit two home runs.

Jessica was so happy that she ran up to her brother and gave him a big kiss on the cheek.

Ugh her brother said. I hope you don't give me a big kiss every time you win a game.

Part C

Zorko watched as Ted and Kevin examined their spaceship.

We'll never get off this planet.

The engines were destroyed when we landed.

Those humans need help.

Zorko   Ted   Kevin

Zorko walked up to Ted and Kevin.

- What did Zorko say to Ted and Kevin?
- Were Ted and Kevin surprised when they saw Zorko?
- Who fixed the spaceship?
- How did they fix the spaceship?
- What did Ted and Kevin say when they climbed into their fixed-up spaceship?

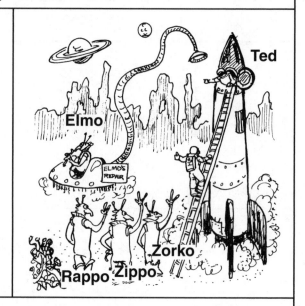

Ted

Elmo

Zorko

Rappo Zippo

| antenna | repaired | crane | crashed | landed |
| explained | damaged | upright |

★ **Check 1:** Is each sentence punctuated correctly?

Check 2: Are there any unclear words in your paragraphs?

Check 3: Did you tell all the important things that must have happened?

Check 4: Did you write at least five paragraphs?

Workbook	Passage				★	
	Check 1	Check 2	Check 3	Check 4	Bonus	Total

Part A

Instructions: Four sentences need commas because they begin with a part that tells when, where, *if, although* or *unless.* Put in the missing commas.

1. Josh and Manuel started to run when the creature closed its eyes.

2. "If you bring your television to my house I will fix it for you," Ana said to Tom.

3. Although she pushed as hard as she could the door didn't move.

4. They live in a house near the river.

5. Tom will miss the party if he is late.

6. While Vanessa fixed a bike Julia talked on the phone.

7. Finally the rain stopped.

Part B

Jim was driving his new car down the road. He drove his car faster and faster. The road got rough and curvy but Jim did not slow down. Down by the river, the road got very bad. It was rough and rocky. All of a sudden, Jim saw a deer in the middle of the road. Jim stepped on the brakes but the car did not slow down. The car swerved and went off the edge of the road into the river. The river was very swift. Jim tried to start the car but the engine was too wet. Jim thought about swimming to shore but the water was too deep and too swift. Jim became very frightened.

Part C

Instructions: Fix up the four unclear words in this passage.

I must destroy. I must destroy.

the robot

This is a disaster.

I told you to be careful when you put the wires together.

Mike

Mike's dog

James

James and Mike looked at the robot they had just built. The robot was standing in the corner of the room holding a fishbowl over its head. It ran away from the robot while the boys stood behind a big cardboard box.

"This is a disaster," he said.

"I told you to be careful when you put the wires together," he said.

The robot had already knocked over a lamp and broken a window. The dog was terrified. It said, "I must destroy. I must destroy."

Part D

Three brothers wanted to buy their mother a computer for her birthday.

Next to the computer store was an office that helped people find jobs.

- How did the boys find jobs?
- How much money did the boys earn?
- Did they spend all their money when they bought the computer?
- What did their mother say when she saw her present?

| stared | extra | sign | earned | bought |
| birthday card | | wrapped | proud | excited |

Check 1: Is each sentence punctuated correctly?

Check 2: Are there any unclear words in your paragraphs?

Check 3: Did you tell all the important things that must have happened?

★ **Check 4:** Did you write at least four paragraphs?

| | Passage | | | | ★ | |
Workbook	Check 1	Check 2	Check 3	Check 4	Bonus	Total

Lesson 40

Test 3

Part A

Instructions: Put the letter *P* in front of each sentence that should start a new paragraph.

Tom prepared to make his first parachute jump. As Tom looked out the door of the plane, he said, "It sure is a long way down to the ground." Then Tom looked at his instructor and said, "I don't think I can jump." "You can do it," the instructor said. As Tom looked down, he replied, "But I sure am scared." "Just close your eyes, count to 10 and jump," the instructor said.

Tom did what his instructor told him to do. He forced himself to take a deep breath and count to 10. Then he jumped. A few moments later, Tom felt a great tug as his parachute opened. As Tom floated down, he said, "This is fun." "Good job," the instructor said to himself as he watched from the plane.

Part B

Instructions: Put in the missing punctuation marks.

1. I don't feel well Jim said to his mother. My head hurts.
2. I hope she sits next to me Alan whispered. She is very smart.
3. That is not my hat Pam said to the teacher. My hat has red and gold stripes.

Part C

Instructions: Fix up the four unclear words in this passage.

Jerry and Alan were friends who worked at a rodeo. Alan was a cowboy. He rode bulls. He was a rodeo clown.

One day, he tried to ride a big wild bull. He held on tightly as the bull jumped up and down. Jerry watched his friend try to ride the bull. All of a sudden, the bull turned sharply and threw Alan into the air and onto the ground. Jerry ran toward Alan. The bull charged toward him. Jerry threw it in front of the bull. The bull ran toward the barrel. While the bull charged toward the barrel, Jerry helped Alan walk to safety.

Part D

Instructions: Four sentences need commas because they begin with a part that tells when, *if, although* or *unless.* Put in the missing commas.

1. I should finish my work by noon if I work hard.
2. Unless the rain stops soon the game will be cancelled.
3. He went to school although he didn't feel well.
4. We will be on time unless we have problems with our car.
5. If she works another hour she will finish repairing the car today.
6. Although he grew two inches over the summer he was still not the tallest in his class.
7. The driver stepped on the brakes when she saw the ducks walking across the street.
8. When she woke up the sky was blue.

Part E

Mr. Jones left his wallet at home when he went to the restaurant.

| embarrassed | money | glared | dishwasher | expensive |

Check 1: Is each sentence punctuated correctly?
Check 2: Did you begin at least one sentence with a part that tells when?
Check 3: Are there any unclear words in your paragraphs?
Check 4: Did you start a new paragraph when another person started talking?

	Passage					
Workbook	Check 1	Check 2	Check 3	Check 4	Bonus	Total

Lesson 41

Part A

Instructions: Four sentences begin with a part that tells when, where, *if, although* or *unless.* Put in the missing commas.

1. If Tom wins the race we will be very surprised.
2. Jerry walked home after he went shopping.
3. On the last day of school we had a party.
4. Although the mouse was hungry it did not go near the cheese that was on the mousetrap.
5. Susan and David went shopping with their mother yesterday afternoon.
6. Near the edge of the swimming pool the pavement was very slippery.
7. The girl who sat next to me in algebra was on the basketball team.

Part B

Instructions: Punctuate the sentences that tell the exact words somebody said.

As Jerry and Tonya were walking home from school, they saw a baby bird sitting on the ground.

Where did the bird come from Jerry asked.

Tonya looked up and said I see a bird's nest in the tree.

The poor bird looks sad Jerry said. Let's put it back in the nest.

I'll climb up the tree Tonya said. You hand me the bird.

While Tonya climbed up to the nest, Jerry carefully picked up the little bird. Then he handed the bird to Tonya. She put the bird into its nest. As they walked home, they could hear the little bird chirping happily.

Part C

Instructions: Fix up the four unclear words in this passage.

Bob took his little sister Leslie to the zoo. At the zoo, they met the zookeeper who was feeding an elephant. While Bob talked to the zookeeper, his sister went to look at it. The bear was in a big pit. To make sure the bear would not get out of the pit, the zookeeper had built it around the pit. Leslie leaned against the fence to get a better look at the bear. Suddenly, the fence broke. Leslie screamed as she tumbled into the bear pit.

They heard the little girl scream. Bob ran over to the fence. The zookeeper climbed onto it and rode to the pit. The elephant picked Leslie up with its trunk and carried her to safety. While Leslie and Bob fed the elephant, the zookeeper fixed the fence.

Part D

Instructions: Fix up the sentences so the word *and* appears only once.

1. Latrell jumped out of his chair and ran to the door.
2. Omar bought shoes and socks and ties.
3. The truck had 16 tires and 2 big horns.
4. He picked up his clothes and made his bed and washed the windows and swept the floor.
5. She opened the door and stepped into the car and turned on the radio.
6. We drank coffee and ate donuts after we came home from the movie.

Part E

The divers got ready to search for a treasure in a sunken ship.

Ray: **We're right over the sunken ship.**

Lisa: **People say the treasure is worth a fortune.**

Mario

Mario   Lisa   Ray

- Did they find the sunken ship?
- Where was the treasure?
- How did they get the treasure into their boat?
- How did Mario's diving suit get torn?
- What did Lisa say?
- What did Mario say?

anchor   face mask   air tank   dove   pressure

jewels   coins   diving equipment   exclaimed   sharks

★ **Check 1:** Is each sentence punctuated correctly?

Check 2: Are there any unclear words in your paragraphs?

Check 3: Did you tell all the important things that must have happened?

★ **Check 4:** Did you write at least four paragraphs?

| | Passage | | | | ★ ★ | |
Workbook	Check 1	Check 2	Check 3	Check 4	Bonus	Total

Part A

The plug for the drain of the bathtub in Mary's house was broken. Nobody could take a bath without the plug because all the water would run out of the bathtub. Mary's father did not know what to do. He tried to make a wooden plug but he could not get the plug to fit quite right. Mary's mother did not know what to do. She bought another plug but it was the wrong size. Mary's brother did not know what to do. He tried to hold his hand over the drain but the water would leak through his fingers. Nobody could take a bath until they found a new plug for the bathtub. Mary knew what to do. She put a small ball in the drain. The ball sealed the drain so that water would stay in the tub.

Part B

Instructions: Six sentences need commas. Put the missing commas in those sentences.

1. Tammy wanted to go to the movies but she didn't have enough money.
2. "If you try hard you'll win the race," the coach said.
3. Although the teacher was sick she came to school.
4. The bell rang just after we finished our math.
5. Jerry had 10 points but he needed 50 points to get the prize.
6. Suddenly the lights went out.
7. Tony will be the champ if he spells this word correctly.
8. Before the bell rang the teacher said, "Today is my birthday."

Part C

Instructions: Fix up the five unclear words in this passage.

Just after the school bell rang, a strange thing happened. It walked into the classroom on its hind legs. The students couldn't believe their eyes. She was making marks on a piece of paper and didn't see the strange animal. The alligator walked toward a seat next to a girl named Ann. "Why is everybody looking at the door?" she asked.

"The new student has arrived," he said.

"Can the new student sit next to me?" she asked. She clapped her hands as she thought about the strange things that might happen that day.

Part D

Instructions: Fix up the sentences so the word *and* appears only once.

1. The baby sat on the rug and played with a bottle.
2. Cedric wrote a letter and read a book and typed a report.
3. Lenora sat down in her chair and began to work.
4. Lisa scored 10 points on Monday and 6 points on Tuesday and 9 points on Wednesday and 15 points on Thursday.
5. He ran upstairs and walked into his room and jumped onto the bed.

Part E

Lisa, Gwen and Nicole were walking home after work.

- How did the women help Mrs. Adams and her son get out of the house?

- Did the women put out the fire?

- Why were Gwen and Nicole wet and dirty?

- What did Mrs. Adams say to the women?

- What did Billy say to Lisa?

| garden hose | yelled | screamed | frightened | flames |
| smoke | against | climbed | hugged | sprayed |

★ **Check 1:** Is each sentence punctuated correctly?

Check 2: Are there any unclear words in your paragraphs?

★ **Check 3:** Did you tell all the important things that must have happened?

Check 4: Did you write at least four paragraphs?

	Passage				★ ★	
Workbook	Check 1	Check 2	Check 3	Check 4	Bonus	Total

Lesson 43

Part A

1. "If you don't have enough money I'll lend you a dollar," Sam said.

2. We left our house at nine o'clock but we still didn't arrive at the bus station in time.

3. Our friend took the bus to New York to visit his dad.

4. On the other side of the room the boys practiced the spelling words.

5. He tried to stay up all night but he fell asleep just after midnight.

6. Steve went to the movies after he ate dinner.

7. As he walked up the stairs Jose said, "I'll see if I have an extra book."

8. We pushed as hard as we could but the rock didn't move.

9. The birds started to fly when they heard the hunter's footsteps.

Part B

Instructions: Put in the missing capitals and punctuation marks.

After Anita and Gwen got home from school they decided to spend some of their money. Let's go to the ice cream store Gwen said to Anita.

"That's a good idea," Anita said. "What are you going to get?"

Gwen said I'll get a strawberry ice cream cone and a chocolate milk shake.

That sounds good Anita said. I'm going to get a strawberry soda and a banana split. The girls ran to the ice cream store. They ordered a milk shake a soda a sundae and a banana split.

The clerk said that will cost eight dollars. Do you have enough money?

"We each have two dollars," Gwen said.

If that's all you have you can each buy one ice cream cone the clerk told them.

Part C

Instructions: Fix up the five unclear words in the passage.

Andy was ironing clothes when he got a call from his friend. Andy put the iron down on the edge of the ironing board and began to talk. While he was talking on the phone, the iron fell into it. Smoke floated up from the basket as they started to burn.

He was hanging a picture upstairs. When he saw it coming through the doorway, he ran downstairs and grabbed it off the wall. He pointed the fire extinguisher at the clothes basket and pushed down the handle. The spray from the extinguisher put the fire out.

Part D

Eric climbed a tree to rescue a cat while Mike and Rosa watched.

- What was in the truck?
- What did Eric's friends say to the truck driver?
- How did Eric get down from the tree?
- Why didn't Eric get hurt?
- What did Eric say to his friends after they helped him?
- How did the cat get down?

| mattresses | piled | yelled | scared |
| tightly | grip | dangled | |

★ **Check 1:** Is each sentence punctuated correctly?

Check 2: Are there any unclear words in your paragraphs?

★ **Check 3:** Did you tell all the important things that must have happened?

Check 4: Did you write at least four paragraphs?

	Passage				★ ★	
Workbook	Check 1	Check 2	Check 3	Check 4	Bonus	Total

Part A

Instructions: Put in the missing capitals and punctuation marks.

Little Blue Riding Hood was skipping down the path with a basket of goodies for her grandma. She came to a big wolf. The wolf said hello, little girl. Where are you going

I am skipping over to my grandma's house with a basket of goodies for her she said.

I'm hungry the wolf said. What kind of goodies do you have

Little Blue Riding Hood put her hand into the basket and said, "I have some eggs." She took out three eggs and threw them in the wolf's face.

The wolf wiped the egg off his face and asked what else do you have in the basket

Little Blue Riding Hood laughed and said, "I have two tomatoes a pie some pudding and four chocolate cream cakes." Before the wolf could grab her she threw all her food at him. While the wolf wiped his face Little Blue Riding Hood skipped on as fast as she could. When she got to her grandma's house she told her grandma why she didn't have any goodies in her basket.

Part B

Instructions: Write an interesting story about Tina and Robert.

Tina   Robert   museum   dinosaur

noticed   Tyrannosaurus rex   triceratops

Check 1: Is each sentence punctuated correctly?

Check 2: Are there any unclear words in your paragraphs?

★ **Check 3:** Did you write at least three sentences that need commas?

Check 4: Did you write at least five paragraphs?

	Passage				★	
Workbook	Check 1	Check 2	Check 3	Check 4	Bonus	Total

Lesson 45

Part A

Instructions: Put in the missing punctuation marks.

Tony, Josh and Kevin were standing outside a computer store. Let's buy our mom a computer Josh said.

"We can't," Tony said. "The computer costs 999 dollars but we have only 400 dollars." The boys stood silently for a while.

Let's get some jobs Kevin said. We can earn the money we need

The boys went to an office that helped teenagers find jobs. The office had openings for baby-sitters gardeners dishwashers and painters. Each boy got a different job.

Every evening, they worked very hard at their jobs. After a month, they had more than enough money to buy the computer.

At their mother's birthday party the boys brought in the present. It was in a box with a red ribbon.

What did you get me their mother asked.

"Open it and see," Kevin said. She opened the package. A big smile appeared on her face.

Thank you she said. "I've always wanted a computer but computers cost so much money. You boys must have worked hard for that computer."

"We did work hard," Josh said. "We wanted to get you something very special for your birthday to show how much we appreciate you."

Part B

Instructions: Write an interesting story about Peter and Jason.

picnic	swimsuits	carried	shortcut	fence
dangerous	rescued	let's	field	through

Check 1: Is each sentence punctuated correctly?

★ **Check 2:** Are there any unclear words in your paragraphs?

Check 3: Did you write at least three sentences that need commas?

Check 4: Did you write at least five paragraphs?

	Passage				★	
Workbook	Check 1	Check 2	Check 3	Check 4	Bonus	Total

Part A

Instructions: Put in the missing capitals and punctuation marks.

Eric was climbing a tree. He climbed to a very high branch. He could see all the houses trees streets and cars in the neighborhood from that branch. "Look at me," he yelled. Eric started to stand up, but then he fell. As he was falling, he grabbed the branch. He hung on to the branch and looked down. Eric wanted to jump but he was scared.

As Eric hung from the tree his friends Rosa, Mike and Tonya walked by. Help me Eric said. I can't hold on much longer.

Hold on Rosa yelled. We'll get you down from there. Rosa, Mike and Tonya looked around for something to help Eric get down.

"A pole, ladder or rope would help Eric get down," Rosa said. They looked for a while but they couldn't find any of those things. After they had looked for several minutes a moving van pulled up.

Let's get some mattresses Mike said. Mike, Rosa and Tonya ran over to the truck. They dragged eight mattresses over to the grass below Eric. They piled the mattresses on top of each other. Mike looked up at Eric and shouted jump when you want to.

Eric jumped. When he hit the mattresses he closed his eyes. Grass dirt leaves shoes and mattresses went flying in every direction. Rosa, Mike and Tonya helped Eric to his feet. He was dirty but he wasn't hurt.

Thanks for helping me Eric said. He put on his shoes. Rosa, Mike, Tonya and Eric walked down the street to Eric's home.

Part B

Instructions: Write an interesting story about Julia, her dad and her brother Ray.

| sunburned | fishing | terrible | caught | never | strange |

★ **Check 1:** Is each sentence punctuated correctly?

Check 2: Are there any unclear words in your paragraphs?

Check 3: Did you write at least three sentences that need commas?

Check 4: Did you write at least five paragraphs?

| Workbook | Passage | | | | ★ | |
	Check 1	Check 2	Check 3	Check 4	Bonus	Total

Part A

Instructions: Put in the missing capitals and punctuation marks.

Lisa, Mario and Ray were looking for a sunken ship. They were riding in a boat. Ray looked at his map. I think we're right above the sunken ship he said. Lisa threw the anchor overboard. Mario Lisa and Ray wore wetsuits. They put on air tanks face masks flippers and breathing tubes.

Lisa stared at the choppy water. She said, "If sharks come near, do you think they will bother us?"

I don't think so Ray said. If they do come, we'll just get back on the ship.

The three divers splashed into the water and started toward the bottom. The water was so dark that the divers couldn't see a thing. They were getting very cold and felt like going back to the ship but they kept looking.

After 20 minutes, Lisa saw something move in the water. It was shaped like other fish but it was very big and moved very fast. After a couple of minutes four more of these things swam by her.

Sharks Lisa said to herself. I'd better warn the others. Lisa swam as fast as she could. She swam by fish turtles plants and jellyfish. She looked for a long time, but she couldn't find Mario or Ray. She was worried. She swam back to the ship. Ray and Mario were already there. They were in the water helping the crew raise a chest on board. The chest was wrapped with ropes. Crew members were pulling on the ropes. Just as Lisa was going to warn the others about sharks, a shark leaped from the water and struck the side of the ship. Everybody let go of the ropes. The chest slipped into the water and sank to the ocean floor.

Mario, Lisa and Ray scrambled on board the ship. "We're safe,"

Lisa said. "Too bad we lost the chest."

We didn't lose it, Ray said. "It's still attached to the ropes. There are the ends of the ropes."

Everybody grabbed the ropes and pulled. Soon the chest appeared from the water. Ray and Mario helped guide it onto the deck of the ship. Lisa pushed the rusty lid open. Everybody stared. The chest was filled with diamonds rubies rings coins and pearls. As the ship started toward home, everybody shouted we're rich. We're rich. We're rich.

Part B

Instructions: Write an interesting story about Ellen and Susan.

| television | noise | suddenly | outside | surprised |

Check 1: Is each sentence punctuated correctly?
Check 2: Are there any unclear words in your paragraphs?
Check 3: Did you write at least three sentences that need commas?
★ **Check 4:** Did you write at least five paragraphs?

	Passage				★	
Workbook	Check 1	Check 2	Check 3	Check 4	Bonus	Total

Lesson 48

Part A

Instructions: Put in the missing capitals and punctuation marks.

There once was a lion who lived in the jungle. The lion was king of all the animals in the jungle the lion was big and mean. When he walked down a path all the other animals hid in the bushes. If one animal saw the king walking down the path that animal would say to his friends, "Hide. The mean lion is coming this way."

One day, a little mouse came up to the lion the mouse said, "I want to be your friend. I am just a little mouse but I will be a good friend."

The lion laughed and said I am the strongest animal in the jungle. Why do I need a little friend like you?

The lion laughed so hard that the mouse fell down. The lion said you are a silly little mouse. Go away. As the mouse walked away he had a tear in his eye. He wanted to be friends with the lion.

One day, the lion took a walk. As the lion walked through the forest, he got a big thorn in his paw. He called to the other animals. He said, "Get this thorn out of my paw.

The elephant tried but he could not get a good hold on the thorn. He said, "I am sorry but I cannot get that thorn out of your paw.

Next, the alligator tried to get a hold on the thorn with his teeth, but he could not He said, "I am sorry but I cannot get that thorn out of your paw

A squirrel a skunk and a raccoon tried. None of them could get the thorn out. After the other animals left the big lion started to cry He said, "My paw is very sore it hurts so much."

Lesson 48   189

When the little mouse heard the crying he ran to see what was wrong. The mouse was very surprised when he saw the lion. The little mouse came up to the lion and said, "I have little paws. I can get a hold on that thorn." The mouse jumped up grabbed the thorn and gave it a jerk. The thorn came out.

The lion began to smile. "It feels good to get the thorn out, he said. "Little mouse, you are my best friend.

If you go to the jungle do not chase after the mice. The mouse you are chasing might be the mouse who has a big friend. That friend is the king of all the animals in the jungle.

Part B

Instructions: Write an interesting story about Mike and his basketball coach.

championship   game   minutes   tied   basketball

Check 1: Is each sentence punctuated correctly?

★ **Check 2:** Are there any unclear words in your paragraphs?

Check 3: Did you write at least three sentences that need commas?

Check 4: Did you write at least five paragraphs?

	Passage				★	
Workbook	Check 1	Check 2	Check 3	Check 4	Bonus	Total

Lesson 49

Part A

Instructions: Put in the missing capitals and punctuation marks.

Janice took her little brother Alan to the store to buy him a birthday present and they spent an hour at the store looking for a special toy car. Alan asked his sister can we stay just a little bit longer? I am sure that I will find the car I want pretty soon.

We can stay as long as you like. I will go up front and look at the magazines while you keep on looking Janice said. Alan looked and looked. Finally, he saw the car he wanted. He picked up the car ran down the aisle and called to his sister.

I found the one that I want he said to his sister. When Janice heard Alan she knew that he was very happy. The car cost more than his sister had planned to spend but she decided to buy it.

Janice and Alan walked up to the cashier and paid for the car. Alan read the directions as they drove home. When they got home Alan began to put the car together. Alan finished assembling the car in 20 minutes. He called to his sister I'm finished putting the car together. Come look at it

You did a wonderful job Janice said to her brother. Let's call your friends and invite them over for cake soda and ice cream. Alan called four boys from his class and invited them over to his house. When all the boys arrived everyone went outside.

Watch me make the car go in circles Alan said to his friends. All the boys took turns playing with the new car. The party lasted two hours and everyone had a good time. As his friends were leaving Alan hugged his sister. Thanks so much. Today was a wonderful day, Alan said to her.

Part B

Instructions: Write an interesting story about James and Sara.

| expensive | fancy | Let's | girlfriend | restaurant | dessert |

Check 1: Is each sentence punctuated correctly?

★ **Check 2:** Are there any unclear words in your paragraphs?

Check 3: Did you write at least three sentences that need commas?

Check 4: Did you write at least five paragraphs?

	Passage				★	
Workbook	Check 1	Check 2	Check 3	Check 4	Bonus	Total

End-of-Program Test

Part A

Instructions: Put in the missing capitals and punctuation marks.

Ken, Ramon and James went to the park to play basketball. When the boys arrived at the park they saw that the basketball court was being used. Vanessa, Karen and Jessica were playing basketball on the court. I hope they go home soon. I don't want to play basketball with those girls Ken said.

That's right said Ramon. We are too good to play basketball with girls. The girls heard the boys talking. The boys did not know that the girls were the stars of the high school team.

Vanessa said let's teach those boys a lesson. She said to the boys, "If you can beat us you can have the court for yourselves."

The three boys and three girls started to play. The boys scored the first basket but the girls scored the next five baskets. The girls were great players. They could dribble pass and shoot the ball very well. After the boys and girls played for fifteen minutes, the score was twenty to two. The girls were winning. The game ended when the girls reached thirty points.

You girls are really good, James said to the girls. Can we play together with you?

That would be fun, Vanessa said. The boys and girls played in the park all day until the sun went down everybody had a great time.

Part B

Instructions: Write an interesting story.

sing   voices   office   beautiful   opportunity

Check 1: Is each sentence punctuated correctly?

Check 2: Are there any unclear words in your paragraphs?

Check 3: Did you write at least three sentences that need commas?

Check 4: Did you write at least five paragraphs?

	Passage				★	
Workbook	Check 1	Check 2	Check 3	Check 4	Bonus	Total